# INTRODUCING DIFFICULT MATHEMATICS TOPICS IN THE ELEMENTARY CLASSROOM

This exciting text for the pre-service elementary teacher provides hands-on lessons for introducing mathematical concepts and skills into the classroom that students find particularly challenging. Each chapter is divided into four sections:

- **The Activity** employs an engaging thought experiment to help the reader "visit a classroom" to understand how the lesson used to introduce the concept or skill would materialize in the class.
- **The Mathematics** provides the necessary mathematical background used in the lesson to make the actual teaching/learning situation comfortable for both the teacher and the learner.
- **The Plan** provides the reader with an actual lesson plan to engage the Activity in the classroom setting.
- **Putting It All Together** pulls the previous sections together with a summary of the chapter as well as further information for making the lesson successful.

By providing models of what excellent lessons on a given topic look like, knowledge of the mathematics involved, and a concrete lesson plan structure, *Introducing Difficult Mathematics Topics in the Elementary Classroom* serves as the definitive mathematics planning vehicle that every teacher will want before they set foot in their own elementary classroom.

# Introducing Difficult Mathematics Topics in the Elementary Classroom

## A Teacher's Guide to Initial Lessons

Francis J. Gardella

 Routledge
Taylor & Francis Group

NEW YORK AND LONDON

First published 2009
by Routledge
270 Madison Ave, New York, NY 10016

Simultaneously published in the UK
by Routledge
2 Park Square, Milton Park, Abingdon, Oxon OX14 4RN

*Routledge is an imprint of the Taylor & Francis Group, an informa business*

© 2009 Routledge, Taylor and Francis

Typeset in Caslon and Trade Gothic by EvS Communication Networx, Inc.
Printed and bound in the United States of America on acid-free paper by Sheridan Books, Inc.

*Library of Congress Cataloging in Publication Data*

Gardella, Francis J.
Introducing difficult mathematics topics in the elementary classroom : a teacher's guide to initial lessons / Francis J. Gardella.
p. cm.
Includes bibliographical references and index.
ISBN 978-0-415-96502-6 (pb : alk. paper) — ISBN 978-0-203-89117-9 (ebook)
1. Mathematics—Study and teaching (Elementary) 2. Logic, Symbolic and mathematical—Study and teaching (Elementary) 3. Curriculum planning. I. Title.
QA135.6.G37 2008
372.7—dc22
2008012555


ISBN 10: 0-415-96502-0 (pbk)
ISBN 10: 0-203-89117-1 (ebk)

ISBN 13: 978-0-415-96502-6 (pbk)
ISBN 13: 978-0-203-89117-9 (ebk)

To my wife, Gail
To my best friend, Gail
To the star of my universe, Gail
To the soul of my soul, forever, Gail

# Contents

# Introduction

Let's begin with a student teacher and teaching mathematics two integral parts of the student teaching experience.

Meet Duane who has been student teaching in Ms. Tollens's classroom for about six weeks. What happens to Duane now is not atypical for those in his station in life, namely, student teacher. Here is his story.

Duane was elated. Ms. Tollens told him that next Tuesday he would teach a mathematics lesson. During his six weeks of student teaching, Duane had done several literacy lessons and a science lesson. Now, he was going to get a chance at a mathematics lesson.

When he saw Leslie he could not wait to tell her. Since her classroom was just down the hall, maybe she could visit and watch his lesson. "I'm going to teach a math lesson next Tuesday," he said somewhat excited. Leslie smiled. "Great," she said, "What are you going to do?"

There are several times in everyone's life where the bubble of elation is attacked by the pins of reality. This was one of those times for Duane. He stood there looking at Leslie as the excitement turned to puzzlement.

That afternoon, he asked Ms. Tollens what she thought would be a good topic for his lesson. "Since we are beginning multiplication, why don't you introduce the idea and prepare the students to begin learning their multiplication facts?" Being a good student, Duane immediately responded, "Okay." As he walked away, he found that his initial excitement, which had turned to puzzlement, had now turned to that empty feeling we get when we have no idea of how to accomplish something we know we truly wish to do.

The scenario above is not unique. Many times, student teachers (as well as new teachers and sometimes veteran teachers) are puzzled as to how to introduce a topic in mathematics. And sometimes, this catches them off-guard. They know the mathematics and they know their students. How can they bring both of them together?

We can assume that Duane, although maybe not a mathematics major, knows his multiplication facts. The question is, "How does he involve the students in their learning without just telling them, 'This is multiplication and here are the hundred facts you need to know.'" (By the way, in some curricula where the facts to be remembered go up to 12 × 12, there are 144 facts. If you include multiplication by zero, there are 169 facts.)

This book gives you some of the answers to Duane's concern (or quandary if it happens to be you.) The book will allow you to "see" mathematics lessons which introduce mathematical concepts to students. In doing this it will support your knowledge of the mathematics involved while helping you to discover how the idea for each individual lesson emerges. Then this is firmed up by having you actually see what a lesson plan for such a lesson looks like.

Each chapter of the book addresses three integrated ideas which teachers need to have in order to create exceptional learning environments in mathematics. These are a model of what an excellent lesson on the topic looks like, knowledge of the mathematics involved, and a lesson plan structure from which the reader can work to deliver the lesson in a real classroom.

In the learning experience, the first question asked is, "What is going on?" So, for that reason, the sequence of each chapter is not in a strictly logical format but more in an instructionally sensible format. First the reader sees what an exceptional lesson on the topic at hand looks like (the Activity). Then we debrief about the mathematics being addressed (the Mathematics). Then you are given the tools to solo (the Plan).

A fourth section of each chapter ties these three areas together with a final section asking you to reflect on what has been done, what you have learned, and how you can implement it. Remember, it is this last element (how you can implement all this) that is most important for you and for your students.

Also, in several chapters, there is a section called "Doing Mathematics." This section asks you to take the ideas and tools used in the activity and practice with them. You, as the teacher need to have not only a clear understanding of the lesson and its sequence, but also be an exemplar in the use of the mathematical tools involved.

## The Activity

In education, as in other professions, many excellent ideas are discussed. Teachers at conferences and through staff development many times hear others discussing exciting work which can make a mathematics classroom come alive. The question that teachers have is, "What does it look like when working with students?" Actually, the real question is, "What would this look like in my classroom?"

The first part of each chapter will help you see this because each chapter begins with what we will call the Activity, what the lesson looks like in a classroom. For each topic, what I have attempted to do is to write a "scene" from a play, the play called "Teaching and Learning Mathematics." In writing these scenes, I have incorporated the knowledge and experiences I have gained from my own teaching at the junior high school level, observing many excellent elementary school teachers, and having conducted demonstration lessons with elementary students when my role as a mathematics supervisor allowed me to show teachers what it would look like in their classroom with their students. As with any play, you imagine the action in your mind. Have your imagination available and see the lesson as if you were a colleague observing the action.

## The Mathematics

All of us have taken mathematics. We know the mathematics of the elementary school. For teaching, the "Mathematics" section of each chapter demonstrates the chosen topic to you, the reader (and then by you, the teacher, to your students) through an investigative, inductive format (with the scene as background) giving you a basis for understanding of the mathematics and then the symbolism and vocabulary which follow. This view of addressing mathematics has proven very successful with many of my students who, as mathematics students in their own right, need to understand the mathematics on a more natural level before the formalism of the content.

About vocabulary and symbolism in mathematics: The mathematical language and symbolic system which we all remember from our schooling is an arbitrary system. By that, I mean that it was developed by people who agreed on certain terminology to make ideas clearer and more concise. However, in order to effectively use the language and symbolism of a system, one must have an understanding of what is being represented. A child with no experience relative to an aard vark would be hard pressed to make any sense out of a word spelled, "a-a-r-d-v-a-r-k" and would certainly not be able to help others learn about such an animal (assuming that the child would even know it is an animal). So, a person without a knowledge of what the symbol ÷ truly represents (and no, it does not represent "goes into"; see chapter 5) would have difficulty assisting a student to understand the concept in a classroom.

It is the goal of this book to give you the fundamental experiential understanding of the mathematics presented in the Activity so that you will go to your students with the power of knowledge, the first basic aspect of an exceptional lesson in any subject.

## The Plan

The final piece of exceptional lessons is the script or lesson plan. A lesson plan must focus on the mathematical, pedagogical, and logistical aspects of the lesson. For this purpose, after we view the classroom and the mathematics, we will study a lesson plan format for you to use. Remember that the purpose of the lesson plan is to allow you to focus on what you want the students to learn, how the lesson will be conducted for them to accomplish this, and the materials that they will need to assist in their learning.

This Plan will include three basic parts:

1. **Objective.** The objective for the lesson will be written in three different formats. The objective will be related to the focal points for K-8 curriculum developed by the National Council of Teachers of Mathematics. There will also be a teacher objective which will specifically state what you expect the students to learn through this lesson. Also, there will be a student objective. This will be an objective written in such a way that students can understand what they are to do and accomplish. This last objective will be written in a language that students can understand and set the basis for their journey to the mathematics you wish them to learn.

2. **Materials.** This will contain a list of the materials you will need to conduct the lesson. These will be the same materials you will read about in the Activity scenarios.

3. **Lesson Sequence.** For each lesson, there will be a beginning and middle. This will be the sequence of actions and activities involved in the lesson. It will be detailed enough to assist you without being so detailed as to make it cumbersome to use in a classroom environment. The final section of the lesson sequence will help you address how the lesson ended while having the students ready to extend it the next day or move on to more in-depth study.

## Doing Mathematics

As part of selected chapters, Doing Mathematics will allow you to practice/review the mathematical focus addressed by using the idea and the materials of the lesson. You may find yourself doing mathematics in a way you have never learned before. That is fine. Mathematics teachers should always be on the lookout for developing a deeper understanding of mathematics and the methods by which it can be demonstrated.

## Putting It All Together

The discussion here focuses on the Activity, the Mathematics, and the Plan as a whole to help you, the teacher, understand how the activity impacts on the students' learning mathematics while answering some of your questions; for example, "How does the activity show the mathematics?"

## Reflections

At the end of each chapter, think about what you have learned both in terms of the mathematics as well as how it can be introduced and represented. The questions in this section are to help you become a reflective teacher, constantly assessing your knowledge of mathematics and your methods of teaching in light of your students. It is a process that you should continue for your entire career in the teaching profession.

## How to Use a Chapter

There are several ways to use this book. I will tell you the way I think works best. First, read the Activity. Try to see the class in your mind's eye as the teacher and the students address the mathematics. Pretend that you are one of the students in the classroom and from this gather some questions that you may have about what a student would think. Write them down and save them for the Reflection at the end of the chapter. And, enjoy!

Then work through the Mathematics section so that you are aware of the topic being addressed in the lesson using the mathematical language adults need to also know if they are to teach properly. If you need to, consult a mathematics textbook for additional work with the topic. There may be times when you wish to refer back to the Activity to make firm in your mind how certain mathematics ideas were addressed.

Now that you know what occurred in the classroom and have a knowledge of the mathematics, read the Plan. Then as you read through the Plan, refer back to the Activity to see why certain ideas are written in the plan and the rationale behind the sequence of these ideas. You may also want to reflect on things you do not see in the Plan and ask, "Why not?"

If there is a "Doing Mathematics" section, approach it as if you were a student. Use the materials even if you do not need them. These sections allow you to review the mathematics of the elementary school while also helping you to become expert in using the physical models that students use in the Activity.

Finally, at the end of the "Putting It All Together section," reflect on your experience. You may also want to discuss the lesson with colleagues if you are teaching or with your cooperating teacher and other students if you are involved in a practicum or student teaching experience. *The more discussion the better.* Discussion of what an excellent mathematics lesson should be enhances the work of all involved.

## About the Book

The aim of this book is have you focus on the teaching of a few but very important concepts/skills in mathematics. I have chosen topics which, in my career teachers have had difficulty understanding and therefore have had difficulty in creating good learning experiences for their students. For the most part, these teachers have not truly understood the mathematics involved and do not wish to pass this on to their students. I offer to you the ideas and lessons which I have and continue to offer to them, lessons that have proven to be successful when teachers take them into their own classrooms.

## About the Chapter Sequence

Before the lessons begin, we take time in chapter 1 to discuss how students learn mathematics, ideas that are important to you and form the basis upon which the book is based.

In using the rest of the book, do not hesitate to revisit chapter 1. It contains the fundamental ideas on which all the lessons are based. With these ideas, you will always remember that the students are the focus of any lesson, the message is the mathematics, and the medium of the message is your teaching activity.

## The Beginning

So, we begin. It is my hope that the entirety of this book will give you the confidence to teach the mathematics with your feet planted firmly in knowledge of mathematics and pedagogy so that your expertise as a motivator of student learning can come to the fore. Your children deserve no less.

# 1

# How Children Learn Mathematics (and Why It Doesn't Happen!)

## Mathematics and Language

The acquisition of the ability to communicate using oral language is a natural phenomenon of the human species. We learn to speak. This acquisition of oral language and the way we learn to link the oral to the symbolic language expressions of reading and writing suggest to me a model for the way children learn and understand the language of mathematics.

The place of language in the learning of mathematics has been discussed for some time. In fact, according to A. G. Howson (1983), it was stated by John Dee as early as the 16th century that books in English would make for

> "better and easier learning and would help students proceed more cheerfully, more skillfully and speedily forward" (Dee, 1570). Yet Dee's thesis that mathematics cannot truly enter a nation's life until it enters the nation's language is, I feel certain, a valid one. (p. 568)

This is pretty heady stuff. Actually, Dee was advocating the use of English language texts in the study of mathematics as opposed to the then prevalent use of texts written in Latin and Greek. (I know many people who today still think that mathematics is mostly Latin and Greek and not because of pi.)

I would like you to consider the validity of the idea of using understandable language in a student's initial learning and further development of mathematics. In one way, it has to do with what Vygotsky called private speech, when children "talk to themselves as they go about their daily activities. This self-talk or overt speech ... does not seem to be addressed to another person ..." (cited in Berk & Winsler, p. 34). In a way, this is the type of communication which all initial learners use, including ourselves, when we learn something new; that is, we use known language in approaching unknown ideas and concepts.

So, as we move on, I would like you to consider teaching mathematics from the point of view of using known language and vocabulary to have students understand mathematical content and then addressing the more formal vocabulary and symbolic formats of mathematical communication. I call this the linguistic/mathematical learning model. (Notice that I told you what it was about before I named it!!!)

Children learn to use linguistic/language structures in stages as they develop proficiency with language from oral to symbolic (reading and writing). There are a set of similar stages by which a learner should develop a knowledge of mathematics and its associated language structure and vocabulary (from the conceptual to the symbolic and formal).

## Learning Mathematics—The Present

In the development of vocabulary in terms of literacy, there is a time frame which begins with introducing children to a new idea and then gradually requires formal use of the word in both oral and written form. Because in many people's minds the study of mathematical ideas is irrevocably linked to the vocabulary used, as if without the formal vocabulary we could not think about mathematical ideas, this time frame is not a part of the learning sequence in mathematics. It happens almost immediately. When a new concept or skill is introduced we see very little time for the use of any communication device at any level other than the formal written/symbolic. If a mathematical concept or skill is to be addressed at a certain grade level, its introduction, development, and use as part of a formal symbolic system all appear in that grade level and in some cases, in the same chapter or chapter subsections.

In the teaching of mathematics, there seems to be a rush to expect children to automatically develop an understanding of a concept after its initial introduction while at the same time expecting students to use the ideas in their most abstract and symbolic forms.

As a counter to this, the teaching/learning structure you will see in all chapters of this book involves having the students first understand the nature of the mathematics and then move on to the symbolic and formal issues. In chapter 2, the lesson is about finding the median of a set of data. You will see how the lesson is first to have students find the middle number and then use it to analyze data. The introduction of vocabulary, such as *median* or *outliers* for the smallest and largest values needs to be accomplished but should be integrated into the end of the second, maybe even the third lesson. The theme in this first lesson and all the other lessons is to give the students one new idea at a time, namely the concept, and having them discuss it using their social language structure before they begin to address the formal symbolic level of the mathematics with its accompanying vocabulary.

Unfortunately, in many mathematics curricula and texts, there is no place for earlier work on a topic at a nonsymbolic/technical level to set the stage for later work on a symbolic level. When some concepts are addressed at a prior grade, it is either done as a one-page insert in the text or at the end of the text in basically a formal symbolic manner.

As an example, look at the previewing of multiplication at the end of Grade 2 as readiness for study in Grade 3. If multiplication is addressed at the end of the program in Grade 2, the content moves quickly from a pictorial representation to the symbolic display of the multiplication facts with the use of × sign as the operator. Although some counting by 2 or 5 or 10 (skip counting) is done during this year as well as in Grade 1 as part of lessons on number patterns, many times it is not related to multiplication addressed here or in Grade 3.

However, let us be clear. It is extremely important that students not just learn but acquire functional use of the formal symbolic representation of mathematics. Students need to know how to communicate mathematics utilizing the system which is well accepted throughout the world. The issue here is not to water down the use of formal symbolic representations, but to call for their learning and use in a proper timeframe, allowing children to understand the concepts and skills involved prior to the development of symbolic representation. And, there are enough years of school to address the symbolic/technical representations in a proper manner.

The model for the lessons in this book places the learning of mathematics and the learning of the related symbolism into proper perspective. As noted previously, the model views the learning of mathematics as a parallel to language development. This demands a period of nonsymbolic development and understanding before the formal written communication conventions of mathematical symbolism are addressed. As in the lesson about division (chapter 5), students must see the process used in problem solving situations before being required to use it to communicate in the conventional symbolic manner. This model as it is demonstrated in all the teaching lessons in this book shows how the mathematics can be addressed without the initial use of the technical vocabulary and symbolic representations. The lessons in this book are for initial teaching, the most difficult part of the teaching process.

## Learning Mathematics: A Continuum

The view that the learning of mathematics is similar to the learning of a new or second language suggests that language learning development forms the basis for the model in the learning of mathematics that is used with the lessons in the following chapters.

Learning takes place in many ways. One of the basic ideas supported by cognitive psychologists such as Piaget and Bruner (cited in Pulaski, 1971, pp. 13–28) is that a person learns along a continuum. Piaget elaborated this theory on four stages: Sensorimotor, Preoperational, Concrete Operational, and Formal Operations and Bruner on three: Enactive (action), Ikonic (imagery), and Symbolic (language). The model for the lessons in this book is adapted from these theories.

During a concrete phase, children begin with the use of physical objects such as Cuisenaire rods, Dienes blocks (base-ten materials), pattern blocks, and then diagrams and pictures to develop and discuss ideas informally, while rising through initial levels of abstraction all moving the student toward the symbolic formats we as adults know.

In this model, abstraction is not seen as a singular level unto itself but as a maturing cognitive process of the learner where the learner moves from an initial phase of abstraction brought on by the interaction with physical models into more complex levels of thinking with symbolism being used as the representation.

It is in a connecting stage that learners begin to relate the physical/pictorial representations of their ideas to conventional symbolism used to communicate mathematics. Moving through levels of abstraction the learners come to a symbolic stage where they can now represent mathematics using the conventional written symbolism and vocabulary. In the connecting stage, learners see the relationship of the modeling they have done in the concrete stage to the symbolic representations by which people communicate mathematically. Figure 1.1, the mathematics learning model, shows the relationship between these stages and the continuum of abstraction involved in the learning of mathematics.

The development of abstraction along a continuum is somewhat different from ideas fostered in the thinking of how one learns mathematics. People mostly think of abstraction in mathematics as being the final stage of learning. But suppose a student can do part of the work with physical models and another part of the work without them.

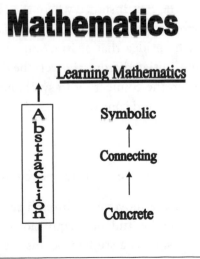

Figure 1.1

Then this student level of abstraction is higher and more cognitively mature than a student who needs the physicality for the entire problem; however, it is not as mature as a student who can accomplish the task with no need of physical models. For example, suppose students are given a problem in which 42 items are shared between two people. Initial teaching will take place using physical models. However, after this, some students will not need to actually have the base-ten blocks (4 tens and 2 ones) in front of them to find that the answer does not require a trade of 1 ten block for 10 ones.

Yet, this same student may need to have materials available if the problem calls for the sharing of 42 apples with three people in order to see that a trade of 1 ten for 10 ones is called for (see chapter 5 for further elaboration on sharing as an introductory model for division). At this level of abstraction, the student would actually take the blocks and use them to establish the need for the trade. Another student whose level of abstraction is even more mature may make the decision about trading before even setting up such physical models, although this student may still need the models to obtain an answer. This last type of advanced decision making certainly is not the highest abstract level of thinking but will occur before any written symbolism is used.

In summary, the level of abstraction used in recognizing the need for a trade before distributing the blocks is certainly more developed than that utilized in the first instance where the child needs to work with the blocks before deciding a trade is necessary. The lessons in this book follow such an idea that abstraction occurs along a developmental continuum initiated from the very beginning of learning. As learners move from the connecting to symbolic stages (see Figure 1.1), they develop the use and control of symbolism in communicating mathematics.

## Communicating Mathematics: A Language Continuum

The focus here is how the movement through the stages of learning mathematics impacts on the student's acquisition of mathematical terminology and symbolism. As a student begins the learning sequence at the concrete stage, the initial manner of communication is the oral/

social level language of the learner, a language of understanding that the student brings into the classroom. It is this language which allows the student to develop realizations and understandings of the mathematics. In the concrete stage, developing mathematical understanding is accomplished without the interference of symbolic structures and technical vocabulary which is as new to the learner as the mathematical concepts involved.

As the learner moves through the connecting stage toward symbolic representation, there is a place then for relating this language of understanding to the development of the language of formalism which is comprised of the symbolism and technical vocabulary which are considered mathematically appropriate. Figure 1.2, where the mathematics learning model becomes the model of mathematics learning/language development, shows this in relation to the stages of learning mathematics as well as the movement along the abstraction continuum.

As stated previously, for many people, the relationship of mathematics to its symbols and vocabulary is one and same. This idea makes it seem that without technical vocabulary and symbols, there is no mathematics. But, one must remember that the symbolism and

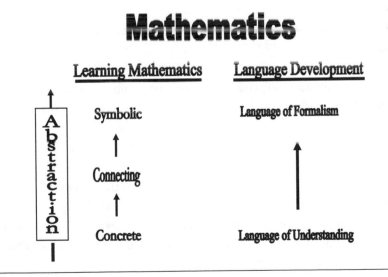

Figure 1.2

vocabulary of mathematics, as with any written linguistic system, are arbitrary not natural; they are developed by people to enable communication to take place. Therefore these systems need a learning experience *after* what they represent is internalized.

The model here at the outset of the learning process develops ideas first and then vocabulary/symbolism. For, at the concrete stage, while developing from a language of understanding, there is little if any formalized mathematical writing in the traditional mathematical sense. Writing done here is in the student's own language, and it is used to explain what is occurring and to communicate a solution to a problem.

As the student moves into the connecting stage, written mathematical symbolism is introduced. But it is done in a way that allows students to substitute a sophisticated, arbitrary symbolic communication system (any formal oral/written language is an arbitrary symbolic system) for one that they already know, their language of understanding and physical representations. The focus then is to enable students to link the ideas which they already understand to the written symbols that are used by the mathematical community to communicate mathematical ideas. It is on this oral to written language continuum that students learn to represent mathematics symbolically and to use the content-related vocabulary for communication.

An example of the mathematics/language learning model in the learning of fractions in the early grades illustrates this. As will be discussed in greater detail in chapter 6, although children in the early grades do understand ideas such as half, the symbol ½ may be seen as two whole numbers (1 and 2) as opposed to one symbol representing a half—as a learner with more developed ability to think in abstract terms, say in Grade 4, may see it. In this case, this representation and interpretation may in fact be setting the stage for later misinterpretation especially in addition, such as ⅔ + ½ where the incorrect answer 3/5 is often seen. In other words, the concurrent teaching of concept and symbolism may be counterproductive to the learning of fractions. It is the case for many of the students that I have trained to be elementary mathematics teachers.

In Figure 1.3, the previously mentioned continuum of oral to written language is placed in the model. Note that the idea of written

# Mathematics

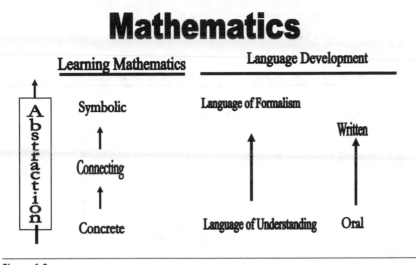

Figure 1.3

language is positioned below that of the language of formalism. This is because students' writing does not begin at the symbolic stage but begins with the use of the language of understanding and develops until the students' knowledge is strong enough to support the cultural symbolic written system with meaning and understanding.

As the student develops mathematical language, vocabulary is a natural consequence. Awareness of conceptual meaning takes place at the language of understanding level with mathematical terminology being introduced in the connecting stage and established in the symbolic stage with the language of formalism. Mathematical vocabulary begins through its use in oral language. However, the formal mathematical symbolism corresponding to this vocabulary should not be introduced at the same time. Just as in the development of language, oral words and meanings come before the writing. Oral vocabulary advances before its use in a written symbolic format.

In geometry, two areas can be used as examples. The concept of congruent figures is basic in geometry from the very first instance. In the early grades, the concept is developed without the vocabulary. However, in the later grades, the term *congruence*, along with its related symbolism, ≅, is introduced simultaneously leaving students to apply not only a new word to a situation, but a new symbolic representation. For many students, this may be problematic.

# Mathematics

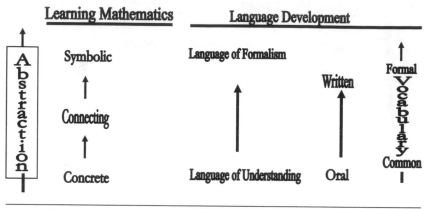

Figure 1.4

Also, the classification of triangles is introduced as a geometric topic and is difficult for many students. This may arise from the thrust of not only having the students focusing on the relationships of sides and angles, but also having them apply new vocabulary of scalene, isosceles, and equilateral (equiangular) in almost the same instance. Although it is very important that the vocabulary and symbolism be established, having this occur during the initial learning of distinguishing various attributes of triangles, adds another layer of "newness" which also may make the mathematics seem more like an exercise in learning words than concepts. Figure 1.4 shows how the development of vocabulary parallels the learning continuum and fits itself into the other aspects of the mathematics/language learning model.

## A Further Implication

Learning takes place at many times in one's life. Much of what is written here is usually taken as what occurs in learning mathematics at a young age. However, this is not the case. Although the Piagetian ideas of sensorimotor and preoperational stages are reserved in education for a young age group, it can and should be premised that, if learning mathematics is parallel to learning a new language, then there must be a stage of learning new ideas in mathematics, no matter the age of the learner, which is akin to the sensorimotor or at least a preoperational stage. For the mathematics/language learning model, this means that learning new mathematics at any grade must begin at a concrete stage.

It is this stage, the concrete, that is skipped in most mathematics learning in the later grades, from the middle school through college, and helps to create the poor results in (and attitude toward) mathematics at these levels. It must be noted that the falloff of success comes when the teaching of new mathematical concepts begins with instruction at a symbolic, written level without even minimal attention to the concrete and connecting stages. I ask you to consider this in light of your own learning experiences in mathematics.

The learning of new mathematical concepts at any age needs to address the language of understanding before progressing to the language of formalism. The model presented in the lessons in this book gives us an opportunity to reformulate our approach to help students begin the learning of mathematics while still maintaining the goal that formal, symbolic mathematics needs to be the end result of the teaching/learning process.

## Summary

The learning of mathematics begins with physical realities and language that are familiar to students and allow them to internalize the concepts. After this is established on a learning/language continuum, the vocabulary and formalism, so important in the communication of mathematics, can be addressed.

Many of us learned mathematics (and remember, we were successful, no matter how you feel about your competence), in which formal symbolism and vocabulary were the realm of initial learning. The lessons here, however, offer an approach in which the students are placed at a stage of understanding when anything new is approached in a common language/physical modeling framework, no matter the learner's age. In this respect, the development of mathematics before symbolism must be addressed with older learners with whom, many times, the mathematics is almost entirely at the formal language, symbolic stage. It is in this that the ideas here permeate the lessons offered in this book and should permeate the entirety of mathematics learning in schools. And therein lies the challenge to the entire mathematics education community especially you, the teacher.

This chapter has been adapted from Gardella, F., & Tong, V. (2002, August). Linguistic considerations in the acquisition and teaching of mathematics. *WORD: Journal of the International Linguistic Association, 53*(2), 185–195.

# 2

# MEDIAN

## Finding What's in the Middle

**The Activity**

**Focus: In this lesson, Ms. Camilla uses the numbers that students choose as the data set and uses the students themselves to "be" the number.**

Ms. Camilla began the lesson by distributing a large index card to each student. She then said, "On the unlined side of the card, you are going to write something. I want you to write it in large block numerals so it can be see across the room. Now, please write a number between 20 and 80 on your card."

While the students did this, Ms. Camilla circulated through the room so that she ended up in the back of the room. When the children were finished, she said, "I need five students to go to the front of the room with their cards." She called out the students as they raised their hands. When the students were in front of the room she said, "Show your cards and without talking, see if you can find which number is in the middle of the five numbers that you have." The students looked around at each other and then finally moved so that the numbers were in order. The person in the middle, Jane, held up her number.

"Good," said Ms. Camilla, "Now, I want everyone to take their journals and write an explanation of what the group did to find the middle number." After a few minutes, she asked for a volunteer and Marshall read. "The group moved around so that the numbers were in order and then they saw the number that was in the middle. "Good," said Ms. Camilla, "Any other ideas?" Several students gave the same interpretation.

Ms. Camilla closed the activity by saying, "So, we say that the five people found the middle number by put the numbers in order and then looking in the middle."

"And now the grand work," said Ms. Camilla. "Here are the rules. You must hold onto your card at all times. Also, you cannot count anything. And last, you cannot speak to each other or to the group. With those rules in mind, the grand work is to find the middle number for the class."

After several moments of concerned looks at each other, one of the students got up and went to the front of the room. With that, others followed and they began to put themselves in order from lowest to highest. As soon as this was done, Elisa began to count the number of people. "No counting," cautioned Ms. Camilla. Elisa slipped back into line.

When Ms. Camilla saw that the students did not know what to do, she said, "Let me help. Since Todd has the largest number and Max has the smallest, I want them to come to the center of the room, shake hands, and go back to their seats." So, Todd and Max did this.

Ms. Camilla asked, "Can anyone tell me what should happen next?" Adrianna said, "Now Sarah and Jennifer are the highest and lowest numbers. So they should shake hands and sit down." "Good observation," said Ms. Camilla. "Go ahead, Sarah and Jennifer. Do what Adrianna said. Todd, what should happen next?" Todd said, "Again the person with the highest number and the person with the lowest number should shake hands and sit down. And that should continue until no one is left."

"Okay," said Ms. Camilla. "Continue until no pairs are left."

And so the students began the pairing off process until Taisha was left standing without a partner to pair off with. "What is Taisha's number?" "56."

"So, 56 is the middle number for this set of data. Thank you Taisha, you may sit down."

"Now, everyone take out their journals. I want you to write an answer to this question and a reason for your answer. The question is, 'Is Taisha's number the middle number for the class?' Remember, you must give a reason for your answer."

When they were done, Ms. Camilla had the students read several of their responses, which were then discussed by the class.

"Now, one more thing: Taisha, would you please take your middle number and stand in the center of the front of the room." After this was done, Ms. Camilla said, "All the people with numbers less than Taisha's, please stand over on her right. Those people with numbers greater than Taisha's, please stand on the left."

The students took their places, those with less than 56 standing on her right and those with more than 56 standing on her left. "Now, Taisha, count the number of people on your right." Taisha counted and said, "Thirteen." Ms. Camilla said, "Now count the people on your left." Taisha counted and said, "Thirteen."

Ms. Camilla said, "So when we find the middle number, what does it do to the group?" Jonathan said, "It gives us two equal groups of numbers, one where all the numbers are higher and one where all the numbers are lower."

"Now," said Ms. Camilla, "One more writing. Go to your journals and write your explanation of what finding the middle numbers does to the group. Then we will discuss these." The students moved to their desks and began writing.

When they finished, Ms. Camilla had some of the students read their responses and a discussion followed.

When this was completed, Ms. Camilla said, "We will now draw a picture of our results." On the board, she shows a number line from 20 to 80. She then asks, "Taisha, would you please go to the number line and draw a line segment above the number line." After this was done, she then asked Todd and Max who had had the largest and smallest numbers respectively to put "dots" on the number line to represent their numbers.

"So, now on our graph, we have the middle number as well as the highest and lowest of our numbers. In our next lesson, we will do more with the middle numbers and also what they can tell us about all of the data."

"Now, for each of your groups, there is a set of small index cards with numbers. Each group is to take their cards, find the middle number, the highest and lowest numbers and then draw the graph."

## The Mathematics

### *The Median*

One of the ways of analyzing data is to write the values in numerical order and then look at the values which appear toward the middle of the data. In fact, a great help in analyzing data is to know the value which has an equal amount of the values on its left and right when the data is written in order from lowest to highest. For example, here is data set containing the number of days of rain in five months: 6, 14, 2, 7, 17. When we write the values in order (2, 6, 7, 14, 17) we see that the value 7 is in the middle, having two values (2 and 6) to its left and 2 values (14 and 17) to its right.

In statistics, this number is called the median. So, in the example above, 7 is the median of the set of data, 2, 6, 7, 14, 17 and we say, "The median number of days of rain for these past five months was 7."

There are two "wrinkles" in finding the median when the data set is not as balanced as the example above.

*Even Number of Values*   Suppose we include a sixth month and it had 11 days of rain. Now we have 2, 6, 7, 11, 14, 17 as our data set. There is an even number of data values and no clear-cut value in the middle. There are three values on the left side of the data set (2, 6, 7) and three values (11, 14, 17) on the right. The median in this case will be the number between 7 and 11 (the two values which form the "middle" of the data set. Since 9 is between 7 and 11, then 9 is the median days of rain.

Yes, it is true that 9 is not in the data set. However, it is considered the median to give us some idea of where the middle of the data is.

**Please Note**: We all know that the easiest way to calculate the middle number between 7 and 11 is to find the mean or average. Do not do this with students at the initial stages of learning. The students need to understand how the middle number is determined and not just find it. Also, it is good to keep the mean and median separated in the learning process since they are similar. When ideas are similar, it is not a good idea to teach them together or in the same timeframe.

*Equal Values* Let's now include a seventh month which also had 11 days of rain. Now our data set is, 2, 6, 7, 11, 11, 14, 17. To find the median, we ask, "What number will have an equal number of values on its left and on its right?" It seems that 11 has this attribute. The "wrinkle" here is that there are two values of 11, and one of them is part of the data set on the left and the other is the median.

But that is all right since finding the median is not what data analysis is about. The median is merely used as an indicator. In this case, one of the values 11 indicates the median of the data set. As I tell my students, there are no job listings for "Median Finders" in the job advertisements. However, there are jobs in "Data Analysis" where finding the median is an aid in analyzing the data.

## Summary

The median is a value which tells us that there are an equal number of data values on its left and right when the numbers are written in order.

1. If there is an even number of data values, the median is between the two "middle" numbers in the data set.
2. If there are equal values near the middle, each is considered an individual data point.

## The Plan

**Lesson Plan**: Beginning lesson for finding the median.

**Teacher Objective**: Students will understand what the median is in a set of data and ways of finding the median.

**Objective for Students**: You will learn how to sort data to help explain what it tells us.

**Materials**: Large index cards which allows students to write their chosen number in large block numbers.

**Warm-Up**: Write a simple explanation of what you mean by "being in the middle."

**NCTM Focal Points 3–5**: Describe the important features of a set of data.

*Beginning Stage*

1. *An index card for each student.* Give each student a large index card and have him or her write any number between 20 and 80, including 20 and 80, on the card. Tell students to write the number large enough so it can be seen across the room.

2. *Small demonstration:* Call three or five students to the front and ask them to find the middle number of this group. Have them explain their process.

*Middle Stage*

3. *Whole class:* Tell the class that during the activity, three rules must be followed:
   a. They must always hold their paper or card
   b. They cannot count to find an answer
   c. They cannot speak to each other

4. *Give the direction:* "You are to find the middle number for all the numbers which have been written by the people in the class."

5. *Allow them time to be uncomfortable and unsure as to what to do:* If someone goes to the front of the room, say, "Good idea, Jeanne," to give the others a hint.

6. *When they have finally lined up, and look satisfied:* Ask, "Okay, what is the middle number?"

7. *Pairing off–high/low:* Help the class use a "pairing off–high/low" strategy where the person with the highest number and the person with the lowest number pair off, come to the center, give a "high five" and then sit down. Then the next two people with the "highest and lowest" numbers do the same thing.

8. *When the middle number is found:* Use a number line marked 20 to 80 to mark the middle number as well as the lowest and highest numbers. (You may wish to use a vertical number line.)

*Final Stage*

9. *Allow the students to work in groups of two:* Give each group a set of data that has a real story line (age of people, salaries, etc.) as a basis, where each data point is written on a separate index card. Have them find the middle number and the end-points and draw number lines to show this.

10. *Put a number line on the board:* When this is completed, have a student from each group put the number line on the board with the median and endpoints marked.

11. *Data comparisons:* Have the students work in their groups to decide on some comparisons of the data.

## Putting It All Together

The lesson allows the students to get the feel for what the median is and how to find it. They physically go through the process of setting the data in numerical order and then establishing the middle number. My graduate students have told me that the process of pairing off is used by students in their elementary school classes. And these young students arrive at this process through their own work and not by being told a rule by the teacher.

The sets of data cards then allow you to introduce the "wrinkles" (see "The Mathematics" section above) as the students use the cards to learn the processes, which they physically carry out. This authentic rehearsal in a guided atmosphere with peer interaction allows the students to talk about the idea in their own words while focusing on the concepts involved (see ideas in chapter 1 about the concrete stage of learning).

The introduction of the term *median* then becomes a judgment call on the part of you the teacher. If the students seem to be moving through the ideas well, then your literacy background tells you that the introduction of the new term may be appropriate. However, if students are having difficulty, the introduction of the formal term at this time may just add to the confusion.

The nature of the work in this chapter is that when the students are called upon to find the median, they can reconstruct what they have learned even to the point of remembering and replicating the "pairing off the data" activity in which they were involved. This type of reconstruction allows all children to be successful in mathematics, even those who do not possess at this time "quick" recall from long-term memory.

## Reflections

### Reflecting on the Activity

1. What were the student-centered attributes of the Activity?
2. How did the teacher help move the lesson along?
3. Who was more active in the lesson, the students or the teacher?

### Reflecting on the Mathematics

4. How many equal groups of data does the median create?
5. If the person with the largest number decided to increase the number by three, would this affect the median of the data set?
6. In this activity, whose number would have to change the median?

### Reflecting on the Plan

7. Why are there two objectives?
8. Why does the plan call for a small demonstration lesson?
9. What role does the teacher plan to play in this lesson?

### Your Reflection

10. Write a reflection of no more than two pages (double-spaced, 12 point type) portraying your thoughts about teaching the concept of the median. Use this to relate your own remembrances of how you learned this idea.

# 3

# ROUNDING

## The Mystery of "Rounding Up for 5"

### The Activity

**Focus: In this lesson, Ms. Ortiz uses a number chart and logic to show students that rules affecting numbers are based on the mathematics involved and not agreements.**

Ms. Ortiz asked the children to work in groups of three. As the students settled into their groups, Ms. Ortiz began to distribute different rows (decades) from a 99-number chart to each group and a pair of scissors. The 99-number chart is like the traditional 100-chart except that the first row shows 0 to 9, the second shows 10 to 19, etc. In other words, it aligns the numbers by families of tens or decades.

Ms. Ortiz distributed the data sheet (see below) and began to explain. "The data sheet asks you to investigate the family of tens that you have been given. Please follow the instructions and I will be around to help if you have any problems. I will give you 10 minutes to complete this."

Ms. Ortiz walked around the room to help students and then wrote headings on the board "Family of units, Family of teens, Family of twenties, etc." She then asked individual members of each group to place their results on the chalkboard identifying the lower numbers and the higher number for their family of tens.

When all the data was on the chalkboard, Ms. Ortiz asked the groups to take three minutes and discuss any pattern that they see. She assigned a student in each group to write down the conclusion for the group.

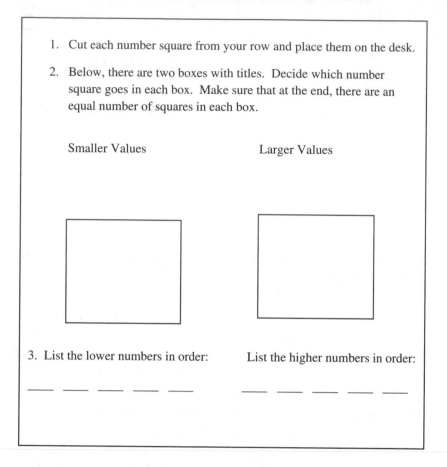

1.  Cut each number square from your row and place them on the desk.

2.  Below, there are two boxes with titles.  Decide which number square goes in each box.  Make sure that at the end, there are an equal number of squares in each box.

    Smaller Values                                    Larger Values

3. List the lower numbers in order:     List the higher numbers in order:

\_\_\_  \_\_\_  \_\_\_  \_\_\_  \_\_\_         \_\_\_  \_\_\_  \_\_\_  \_\_\_  \_\_\_

Ms. Ortiz asked Isaac to read his group's conclusion. "All the lower numbers end in 0, 1, 2, 3, or 4. All the higher numbers end in 5, 6, 7, 8, and 9." "Great," said Ms. Ortiz, "Now here is why this pattern is important." She goes to the flip-chart and uncovers the problem: "'Joshua earned $64 in one week and $28 in the next week. About how much did he earn?' Now we could add these but we just want to find out about how much Joshua has. Here is one way of doing this."

"$64 is in the lower 60s so we change it to the nearest 10, namely $60. So we use $60 instead of $64. Since $28 is in the higher 20s we change it to the nearest 10, which happens to be $30. This will now make it easy to add it to $60. So now we have $60 and $30. When we add them, we get $90. So, the sum of $64 and $28 is about $90."

"Now, in your groups, add $64 and $28 and see how close to $90 your answer is. You have two minutes."

After the groups finished their work, Ms. Ortiz asked for the answer and Jonathan answered, "Two dollars." Ms. Ortiz stopped for a moment and said, "Why is that not an acceptable answer, Jonathan?" Jonathan coyly said, "Because I did not answer in a complete sentence." "Try it again," said Ms. Ortiz. Jonathan responded, "The real answer is $2 more than the 'about' answer."

"Thanks, Jonathan. And since the real total is only $2 from the 'about' total, it helps us to see if our real answer makes sense."

"What you just did is round the amount to the nearest 10 before adding. It gives you an answer that is near the real answer. See how it works with this problem." Ms. Ortiz uncovers problem 2 on the flip chart. "Sally saved $55. For her birthday, she received another $32. About how much money does she now have?" "Try it alone to find what Jonathan called the 'about' answer and the exact answer. Compare them to see if they are close. Then explain your answers in your group."

When time was up, Ms. Ortiz called on Rachel. Rachel said, "$55 is in the upper 50s. So I used the nearest 10 which is $60. Since $32 is in the lower 30s, I used 30. Then I added $60 and $30 and got $90. So, Sally received about $90 for her birthday."

"Great," said Ms. Ortiz. "Now, we are going to use this to see about how much we spend when we shop in some of the catalogs I have in the back of the room. I want you to use the idea of rounding and see how close you come to the actual total that you spend."

## The Mathematics

What you have read about in Ms. Ortiz's class may be very different from the way you may have learned about rounding numbers in elementary school. You may have been told that for the numbers ending in 1, 2, 3, and 4 you round down to the nearest 10 and for those ending in 6, 7, 8, and 9 you round up to the nearest 10. For 5, it is an agreement (you may hear that a lot in mathematics) that you round up to the nearest 10. Well, you should round up when the ones' digit is 5. But it is because of the mathematics and not because of an agreement.

For our discussion here, let's use the 40s as our family of tens. The mathematics of the real number line is that there are just as many numbers between 40 and 44.99999 ... as there are between 45 and 49.9999.... In other words, the lower 40s contain the whole numbers 40, 41, 42, 43, and 44 while the higher 40s contain the whole numbers 45, 46, 47, 48, and 49.

So, when you are working with numbers between 40 and 50 and you want to round to the nearest 10, you round the numbers in the lower half of the 40s to 40 and the numbers in the higher half of the 40s to 50.

In a similar way, you can round to the nearest hundred. For example, if you are working with the numbers between 200 and 300, then there are 50 whole numbers from 200 to 249, the lower 200s. Then there are 50 whole numbers from 250 to 299, the higher 200s. If you want to round 223 to the nearest hundred, you would round it to 200 since 223 is in the lower 200s. If you round 250 to the nearest hundred you would round it to 300 since 250 is in the higher or upper 200s.

In doing this, you must keep in mind that if you count the whole numbers between 50 and 59, there are 10 of them. (This may give you a different if not uncomfortable feeling since you have usually thought of numbers from 51 to 60 and not 50 to 59.) There are five numbers in the lower 50s (50, 51, 52, 53, 54) and five numbers in the higher 50s (55, 56, 57, 58, 59). Using the same type of thinking, there are 50 whole numbers from 600 to 649 and 50 whole numbers from 650 to 699.

## The Plan

**Title**: Beginning lesson for learning skill of rounding for estimating.

**Teacher Objective**: Students will learn to round numbers to the nearest 10 and sums for estimation.

**Objective for Students**: Learning one way to make sure your answer makes sense.

**NCTM Focal Points 3–5**: Develop and use strategies to estimate the results of whole number computations and to judge the reasonableness of such results.

**Materials**: Data sheet; strips of decades for each group; catalogs; scissors.

**Problem 1 on Flip Chart**: "Joshua earned $64 in one week and $28 in the next week. About how much did he earn?"

**Problem 2 on Flip Chart**: "Sally saved $55. For her birthday, she received another $32. About how much money does she now have?"

**Warm-Up**: Write a short explanation for this statement: "Joshua said that he had about 30 cents in his pocket."

*Beginning Stage*

1. Use the warm-up as a point of discussion to have students discuss what the focus of estimation is.

*Middle Stage*

2. Give explanation of number strips.
3. Explain the use of the data sheet.
4. Have students complete the activity with the strips and data sheet.
5. Have a representative from each group place the responses for the lower and higher numbers for each decade.
6. Ask students what patterns they see and reinforce the movement of lower and higher numbers.
7. Give the students the first problem on the chart and work in groups to solve it.

*Final Stage*

8. After discussing the solution, have them do another problem as individuals and then discuss it in the groups.

## Putting It All Together

Rounding as one skill in developing estimation is a major part of developing number sense in students. It is also very important in the development of quantitative literacy. The reason for this is that estimation of sums, differences, and products can be done in several ways. It calls for the person to be "flexible" with numbers and operations and use the conceptual basis for working with numbers in prescribed as well as individual and yet correct ways. Rounding is one way of estimating and, to date, the most popular in mathematics curriculum. This may be because it is so procedural and rule based.

However, you now know that the idea that rounding as a rule or agreement (as taught in many programs) is not accurate. The accurate idea has to do with the mathematics of real numbers which is a very deep and complex topic. But, when you begin a topic as complex as this with a major subset, the whole numbers, it allows you and your students to see that it makes sense.

It is very important at any stage of mathematics to insure that your students see mathematics not as arbitrary and rule/agreement driven but as a way of communicating based on good reasons.

## Reflections

*Reflecting on the Activity*

1. What were the student-centered attributes of the Activity?
2. How did the teacher help move the lesson along?
3. Who was more active in the lesson, the students or the teacher?
4. Why did Ms. Ortiz not use words such as *estimating* or *approximating* in this first lesson?

*Reflecting on the Mathematics*

5. What would be the "lower" and "upper" numbers between 80 and 89?

6. Why would it be better for students to have an understanding of rounding and not just the rule?
7. How would the idea behind the lesson help with helping students learn how to round to the nearest thousand?
8. Put yourself in the place of Ms. Ortiz. How would you change the lesson or any of its parts to fit your personality better?

*Reflecting on the Plan*

9. How do you think the warm-up would help in readying the students for the lesson?
10. What did Ms. Ortiz do before the lesson to be ready for the lesson?
11. Could she have written the problems on the chalkboard? What would this have done to the rhythm of the lesson?

*Your Reflection*

12. Write a reflection of no more than two pages (double-spaced, 12 point type) portraying your thoughts about teaching the concept of rounding. Discuss how it fits into the learning model discussed in chapter 1.

# 4

# SKIPPING MULTIPLICATION (OR AT LEAST THROUGH IT)

**The Activity**

**Focus: Ms. Wengler involves students in a system for learning multiplication facts using patterns which allow them to reconstruct their learning.**

Ms. Wengler taped a strip of paper on the wall. The strip was about 12" wide and 4' long. On it, written vertically were the even numbers from 2 to 20 (see chart on next page).

She said, "Here are the numbers from 2 to 20. In your groups, decide on some ideas that would describe this list. You have two minutes."

At the end of the time, she called on Fred, the reporter for his group. "The list is counting by 2s up to 20. There are 10 numbers on the list."

"Good, and that is a simple as it can be. The pattern is by two and there are 10 of them. What we are going to do today is look at other patterns for counting." As she said this, Ms. Wengler uncovered a piece of chart paper which had the objective for the day.

Learn to count by patterns of numbers. Today's number is 3

Ms. Wengler taped a strip of paper on the wall. The strip was about 6" wide and 4' long. She then handed one of the students, Andy, a chip. She explained: "The chip I gave Andy will be used by his table to create a list of numbers. Rachel (a student at another table) can I ask you to record the numbers on the strip. Here is a marker. Now,

| |
|:---:|
| 2 |
| 4 |
| 6 |
| 8 |
| 10 |
| 12 |
| 14 |
| 16 |
| 18 |
| 20 |

the other three people at Rachel's table come over to Andy's table with your chairs." This then made seven people in Andy's group.

When Rachel was at the strip, Ms. Wengler explained the rules for developing the set of numbers. "What Andy will do is begin by mumbling the number 'one' and then passing the chip. Since the number is mumbled, Rachel does not write anything on the paper. The next person will mumble the number 'two' and pass the chip. The next person, Cara, will yell the next number and that's the one Rachel will write on the board. The next two people will mumble their numbers and then there will be a yell. That will be you, Bill." Bill smiled and rubbed his hands together in anticipation. "When everyone at this table has had a turn, that will be at you, Dalton, you will pass the chip to Martha at her table. That is the way we will continue around the room."

"When do we stop?" asked Samantha. "Based on what we did before with counting by twos, how many numbers should Rachel have on the chart for us to stop, Tom?" asked Ms. Wengler. "Ten." "Good.

So when Rachel has heard 10 shouts and has written 10 numbers, she will tell us to stop. Then we will see what we have."

"So, let's try it. Remember, the pattern is two mumbles and a yell. Go."

Andy mumbled, "One." Reggie mumbled, "Two." Cara yelled, "THREE!!!"

Everyone in the class laughed and looked at Ms. Wengler. She said, "Excellent, Cara. Write it, Rachel! Let's go on. And get ready Bill." Stephanie mumbled "Four." Traci mumbled "Five." Bill, with much gestural fanfare yelled, "SIX." Again, there was laughter from the class.

"On that note, let us continue." said Ms. Wengler. The next student, Dalton mumbled, "Seven" and handed the chip to Martha at the next table who mumbled, "Eight" and then handed the chip to Reggie yelled, "Nine."

Ms. Wengler had them continue around the room until Wanda yelled, "Thirty."

Before the next person could speak, Rachel said, "Okay, we have our 10 numbers."

Ms. Wengler collected the chip from Wanda and said, "In your groups, I want you to decide why 30 might be a good place to end." She helped the students from Rachel's table move back to their group and then moved through the room and monitored the discussion.

When she called for recorders, Amy said, "It was the tenth time there was a yell like with two. Did that have something to do with it?" "Good," said Ms. Wengler, "Anyone else?" "Rachel ran out of room on the chart," said Bill. The class laughed a little.

"Well, she did," said Ms. Wengler, "So we had to stop. But that is not the mathematical reason. I think Amy had a good idea. Now, discuss in your groups where we would stop if the first yell was at four and then we may see another pattern forming."

After a few minutes, Cara raised her hand and said, "We think you would stop at 40 because that would be the tenth yell." "Sounds like a good idea," said Ms. Wengler. "Next week when we do fours, we'll check it out."

"So, let's look at the chart. Take your notebooks. On the inside of the back cover, on the left side, write the column for two and then make a space and write the numbers for three in a column as Rachel did it on the board. This is so you can find them easily when you need them."

"When will we need them?" asked Bill. "Let's wait until everyone has written the numbers in their notebooks, including you, Bill," Ms. Wengler said. Bill smiled, opened his book and wrote.

As the students were writing, Ms. Wengler placed seven paper bags on the front table. When the class was done writing, she called for attention and uncovered a problem on the chart paper. It read, "Suppose there are three apples in each of these bags. How many apples do you have in all?" She then said to the class, "Work in your groups to find out how many apples you would need and be ready to state how you arrived at your answer." After a few minutes, she called for some responses.

"We added three to itself seven times. We got 21 apples." said Sara. "We just counted seven steps down the list on the paper in the front of the room. The seventh number is 21." said Rachel.

"Great," said Ms. Wengler. "Tomorrow we will look at other problems to solve using adding threes like Sara's group and using the pattern of threes like Rachel's group. Homework pads please." With some groaning, the students took out small homework books. "Tonight, I want you to recite the list of threes three times. Come in tomorrow ready to use it to do some problem solving." Fred said, "But I know these already." Ms. Wengler said, "Fred, do what you need to do to be ready for tomorrow's work."

"So, now put away your mathematics notebooks and clean up before we go to lunch."

## The Mathematics

Multiplication is one of the most important concepts that students learn in the elementary school. It sets the basis for problem solving in the real world as well as fundamental ideas in the learning of higher mathematics from algebra to calculus and beyond. It is one of the first major topics in which the idea of patterns becomes functional in learning and using mathematics.

One of the basic ideas of multiplication is that it is "group addition." If you have to add 7 + 9 + 6, you need to actually take each addend and "add." However, if you have to add 6 + 6 + 6, you have an opportunity to discuss the pattern when 3 sixes are added together. Notice here that the number focused on, six, is written as a word while the number of these that you have is written as a numeral.

Multiplication is an idea in which you have something (quantitative noun) so many times (quantitative adjective). The idea of "3 trucks" denotes physical trucks and there are 3 of them. The truck is the noun showing what exists and the 3 is the adjective showing the number of trucks.

In multiplication, the idea of 3 × 6 means 3 sixes. Six is, in a sense, a quantitative noun denoting a set amount. The 3 denotes how many of these amounts we have. So, we can call 3 a quantitative adjective.

This idea of "quantitative noun" and "quantitative adjective" also has relevance in dealing with a geometric model for multiplication. The geometric model involves a grid (like a piece of graph paper) in which a section is bordered. Here is an example of 3 × 6.

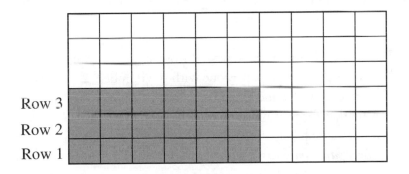

In the grid, we have 6 gray squares in each row. A row of 6 gray squares is our quantitative noun. There are 3 of these rows. Since the 3 describes the number of gray rows, it is the quantitative adjective. So, 3 rows of 6 gray squares each gives us 6, 12, 18; 18 squares in all. (In a similar fashion, you could say that there are 6 columns each containing 3 squares. In this case, the 6 would be the quantitative adjective and the 3 would be the quantitative noun. How do you decide? It is the context of the use that determines which is the quantitative noun and which is a quantitative adjective.)

Notice that although this is a geometric model for multiplication, the idea of the adjective and the quantitative noun (and the skip counting) still plays a role in finding the product.

In dealing with multiplication, we must never lose sight of this idea. Even when multiplying large numbers, one of the numbers must always be a quantitative noun telling us an amount and the other must always be a quantitative adjective telling us how many of these amounts we have. Also, with fractions, such as ½ × ⅓, we have ⅓ of a quantity and we are taking ½ of it. Whether we use area models or linear models (see chapter 6) the idea of a quantitative adjective linked to a quantitative noun still holds.

### The Plan

**Teacher Objective**: To introduce students to the process of skip counting and the answers to multiplication facts.

**Objective for Students**: On chart paper: Learn to count by patterns focusing on 3.

**NCTM Focal Points 3–5**: Describe, extend, and make generalizations about numeric patterns.

**Materials**:

Chip or other item to be passed from student to student.

Two strips of chart paper, one with the numbers 2 to 20 written vertically and the other blank.

A marker for writing the numbers on the chart paper.

7 small lunch bags.

*Chart paper with lesson objective*: Learn to count by patterns of numbers. Today's number is 3.

*Chart paper with the statement*: Suppose there are 3 apples in each of these bags. How many apples do you have in all?

*Beginning Stage*

1. Put up the chart paper having the numbers 2 to 20.
2. In their groups have the students discuss what is happening.

3. Have a discussion with the class about the idea of counting by 2.
4. Display the Objective for Students.

*Middle Stage*

5. Put up the blank chart paper (make sure it is not too high).
6. Choose Rachel to write the numbers and begin with Andy's table. (Have Rachel's table join Andy's.)
7. Explain the passing of the chip. Begin.
8. When this is over, discuss the column of numbers (3 to 30).
9. Have students in groups discuss the ending at 30.
10. Students write a list on the inside of the back cover of their notebooks.
11. Then have the students discuss where would be a similar ending place if they used 4 as the number.

*Final Stage*

12. Place bags on table. Give problem (3 apples in each bag. How many apples altogether?) Have students solve problem in groups and then discuss the answer.
13. *Homework:* Ask students to recite the list of threes 3 times.

## Putting It All Together

One of the major issues in elementary school mathematics is learning multiplication facts. Read most critics of mathematics education and somewhere in the writing there will be a reference that today's students do not know their multiplication tables.

Now, whether all students in the past did in fact know the multiplication tables or not cannot be determined since there were no assessments as there are today. But, is it a fact that students today do not know their multiplication tables? I don't care.

Now that you have recovered from that statement, let me tell you why. Multiplication tables are a formalized system for showing all the multiplication facts. And, before you can formalize something, you must know it (review chapter 1 for details on this).

It is more important for students to know their multiplication facts than to know their multiplication tables. The simple reason is instructional. There are many ways of focusing on multiplication facts. One of them appeared in the Activity in this chapter. However, with the multiplication tables, there is only one way to address them—memorization. And, I ask, where do we teach students how to memorize before we ask them to memorize this vast amount of information (upwards of 100 facts)? The answer is we do not. No school has a section of the day devoted to teaching students how to memorize and yet, for multiplication, some educators pose it as the chief skill in the learning.

The Activity here gives the students two ideas. First, through the use of "3" they develop the answers to the multiplication facts for "3." Moreover, through the procedure, the students are given a system by which they can develop and reconstruct the multiplication facts for any other number. (Obviously, having them do this for numbers through 10 is sufficient. However, they can challenge themselves to count by 25 when dealing with money, 12 when dealing with number of pieces in dozens, etc.)

In a system of rote memory, there is an assumption that the memory will not fail. No college graduate will ever say that cannot happen. (Remember some exam you had?) Memory does fail. And for the student who needs assistance in reconstructing facts when this occurs, the memorization pedagogy leaves them in harm's way.

One last thing: Over the course of grades 1 and 2, students can learn to skip count by 2, 3, 4, and 5. From this, two things occur: First, they enter 3rd grade knowing all the answers to the "tables" from 2 to 5. So, the teacher's job is to formalize the idea of multiplication and not totally focus on the answers.

Second, this leaves only 10 more multiplication facts to learn. Only 10? What about all the facts in skip counting by 6? Well, 4 of them ($6 \times 2$, $6 \times 3$, $6 \times 4$, and $6 \times 5$) are already addressed in dealing with smaller numbers 2 to 5.

When you actually come down to it, the facts still to be mastered are:

$$6 \times 6 \quad 6 \times 7 \quad 6 \times 8 \quad 6 \times 9$$
$$7 \times 7 \quad 7 \times 8 \quad 7 \times 9$$
$$8 \times 8 \quad 8 \times 9$$
$$9 \times 9$$

Ten facts to be learned in an entire 3rd and 4th grade is not overwhelming, and this is based on my experience in schools where it has occurred.

## Reflections

*Reflecting on the Activity*

1. How did Ms. Wengler keep the students involved throughout the lesson?
2. Discuss how Ms. Wengler allowed the students to interact with each other.

*Reflecting on the Mathematics*

3. That students forget is a known problem in education. How does the skip counting format for multiplication help students when they do forget their facts?
4. Explain how teaching students the multiplication facts for the "3-times table" using skip counting enables them to learn other sets of facts even before they are addressed in your classroom.

*Reflecting on the Plan*

5. What would have been a lesson objective for the students which the students may not have understood? Explain why.
6. How does this lesson adhere to the NCTM Focal Point to make generalizations about numeric patterns?

*Your Reflections*

7. If you were the teacher, would your next lesson be about skip counting by 4? Explain your response.
8. Summarize your thoughts on the difference between having students memorize the multiplication tables and students learning the process of skip counting.

# 5

# LEARNING TO USE DIVISION

## The Activity

**Focus: Mr. Servon uses a sharing model and physical models to begin to have students understand division as a sharing process and sets up a model from which to introduce the division algorithm.**

The students moved into their groups as Mr. Servon distributed the base-ten blocks and five index cards to each student. He then displayed the following problem on the overhead projector: "Marisa has 4 bags of 10 jelly beans and 5 single jelly beans. She wants to share them with two of her friends and herself. How many jelly beans does each person get?"

"In your group, help the constructor set up the problem with the cards acting as the people and the base-ten blocks acting as the jelly beans. Now, talk about solving the problem and then solve it. Again the recorder is to take notes on what the group decides to do."

As the students began to work, Mr. Servon walked around the room to help where it was needed. As the students began to finish, Mr. Servon collected the recorders reports.

He then asked for Greg's group to report to the class. Mr. Servon has seen that their group had worked the problem out in a good manner.

Stephanie stepped to the overhead projector and used the base-ten blocks to demonstrate. Stephanie began by showing 4 tens and 5 ones on the overhead. "Here are my jelly beans." She then drew three circles at the bottom of the overhead and said, "These show me and my two friends who are going to share the jelly beans."

"Now, each one of us gets 1 bag of 10 jelly beans. So, I put 1 10-bar in each circle. That leaves 1 bag of 10 and 5 jelly beans left to share. Since we cannot share out the 1 bag of 10, we open the bag and place the 10 jelly beans with the other 5. To do this with the blocks, I trade the 1 10-bar for 10 ones. This gives us 15 jelly beans. Now, when we share these jelly beans, I can place 5 jelly beans in each circle. Since there are no jelly beans to share, we have finished sharing. When we look in each circle, we see that there is 1 10 bar and 5 ones. So, each person will receive 15 jelly beans."

Mr. Servon called for the students' attention. "Notice that the answer is not 15. We do not have just one group of 15. According to Stephanie, we have three groups of 15. So, when you write your answer, please use a complete sentence and state what you mean."

"Can anyone add to this?" asked Mr. Servon. Taisha asked, "What happens if there are jelly beans left over after they are shared?" Mr. Servon said, "Taisha asked what you do if there are jelly beans left over after you share them. You have two minutes in your groups to answer Taisha's question. Go!!!"

The groups began to discuss the problem and reporters began to raise their hands. "Martha?" asked Mr. Servon. Martha said, "Well, if there are one or two jelly beans left over, they can be cut up and then each person will get pieces of the jelly beans. If there are three or more, then each person can get more jelly beans."

"Now, that's important" said Mr. Servon, "and we will see more of this tomorrow. But right now, let's solve some more sharing problems."

"I have six boxes in front of the room marked A to F. Each box has a problem sheet in it. Your group will work on problems A to F one problem at a time. As you take a problem, please remember to put your group's name on it. Then, as you complete a problem, put it in the correct box and then take the next problem. To make it easier, I will distribute the problem from box A. Remember, as you finish, the materials person brings the problem up, puts it in the correct box, and takes the next problem. Here is problem A. We will review these tomorrow."

## The Mathematics

Division in reality has two contexts. First, I can have a lot of stuff and want to share it with others. Let's call this example A: Sally and

2 friends are going to equally share 45 seashells. How many seashells will each person receive?

A second context is this: I have one large item and want to see how many pieces of the same size I can make from it. Let's call this example B: Jonathan orders a 24-inch long sub sandwich. How many 4-inch pieces can he cut from this sub?

Problems like example A should be used first to introduce division. One reason is that they lend themselves to physical modeling and perception more easily than those like example B. Also, problems like example A, called the sharing (or partitioning) model of division make the transition to the standard algorithm for division used in the United States easier to explain.

Note: For those of you who are wondering why I mention the United States, I have met students from other countries who use a different model. I will show this at the end of this section.

So, let's discuss the division algorithm and how it can be obtained from "sharing" problems. In the Activity above, the children in Mr. Servon's class were sharing 45 jelly beans packaged in packs of tens. So there were 4 tens and 5 ones. The chart below shows how the steps of the process with the tens and ones lead to the writing of the algorithm focusing on the meaning of each symbol and its place in the algorithm (see Figure 5.1).

In the diagram you can see how the language in the left column matches the movement of the materials in the center column and how this is recorded with the algorithm in the right column. So, division has two contexts, one of which can then be used in the initial stages of learning to show the standard algorithm.

**About the Note:** Above there was a note about the algorithm. It is agreed in many countries that $3\overline{)45}$ means 45 divided by 3. However, in some places, such as Peru and the Ukraine, this same division, 45 divided by 3 would be written $45\overline{)3}$. You can understand the confusion of students when trying to study under one system having initially learned with another system, or when parents educated in these countries try to assist their children with the work.

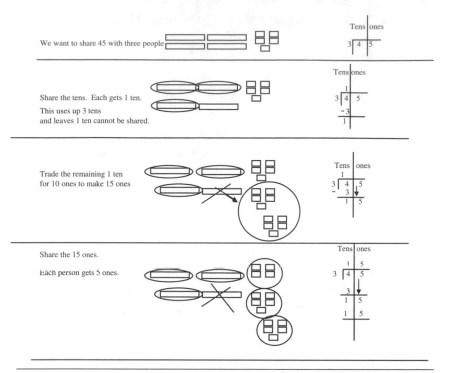

**Figure 5.1**

## The Plan

**Title**: Introducing division as a sharing process.

**Teacher Objective**: To introduce students to division as a sharing process.

**Objective for Students**: Solve problems by sharing equally.

**NCTM Focal Points 3–5**: Select appropriate methods and tools for computing with whole numbers.

**Materials**: Base-ten materials, index cards, overhead projector, and prepared transparencies, problems on strips of paper marked A to F, Boxes for the problems marked A to F.

**A to F, Boxes for the Problems Marked A to F**:

>　Problem A: Sam, Bill, and Katie get 48 crayons to share equally. How many crayons does each person get?

>　Problem B: Three teams will share 42 baseballs. How many baseballs will each team receive?

Problem C: A librarian gives 24 books to two students to share. How many books did each student receive?

Problem D: Marisa, Millie, and Mike are sharing 4 dimes and 8 pennies. How much money does each receive?

Problem E: For the two 4th grade classes, Ms. Vasquez bakes 36 cupcakes for the party. How many cupcakes will each class have for the party?

Problem F. Joshua, Heidi, and Mel share 56 shells for a project. How many shells does each student receive?

### Beginning Stage

1. Distribute base-ten materials and cards. Call students' attention to the problem concerning Marisa and her friends. Give students five minutes to construct a solution.

### Middle Stage

2. Choose a student to report on a group's work. Have a student from the group go to the overhead projector and relate how the group solved the problem. Emphasize that the answer (15) represents 3 groups of 15 and not just 15 ones.

### Final Stage

3. Distribute problems one at a time. Remind students to write the group name on each problem. As a group completes a problem, have them place it in the solution box for that letter and then take another problem. Give students the rest of the mathematics time to complete the problems.

## Putting It All Together

Division is considered one of the more difficult procedures for students to master. One reason is that the traditional teaching of the algorithm does not incorporate what is actually occurring in the process. Students (as may have happened to you) are simply shown the algorithm, told where to place certain numbers, and how to use (DMSBSO): Divide, Multiply, Subtract, Bring Down, Start Over.

The lesson here develops the understanding of the process (what is going on) which can then lead to a recording of the results (the algorithm). It is this type of instruction that you should strive for in all of your mathematics teaching. Algorithms from rote memory mean nothing and are easily forgotten. Processes without a firm direction in how to record the results do not provide students with efficient communication devices.

As you can see, the students not only know place value but use it as a computational tool. It is the basis of our counting as well as the basis for our operations (addition, subtraction, multiplication, division) with whole numbers. Place value together with base-ten materials forms the foundation for leading students to understand and communicate mathematically.

*Doing Some Mathematics*

In the lesson, Mr. Servon created six problems for the students to solve. Using a set of base-ten materials, do these problems which are listed in the Materials' section of the Plan.

## Reflections

*Reflecting on the Activity*

1. What was the major idea that Mr. Servon was trying to have the students learn?
2. How did Mr. Servon keep the students involved in the lesson?
3. Besides sharing as a division model, Mr. Servon introduced the idea of what happens when the quotient is not a whole number. How did he do this?

*Reflecting on the Mathematics*

4. Why is it important for students to use physical models in developing an algorithm?
5. Why is it important for student to develop an algorithm for an operation such as division?

*Reflecting on the Plan*

6. How did Mr. Servon plan to keep the students actively involved in the lesson?
7. How would you modify the lesson to introduce a situation which involved "hundred" such as "There are 345 jelly beans to be shared with 3 students."?

*Your Reflections*

8. Place yourself in the role of the teacher. What are the classroom management tools you use to keep the students on task?
9. How does informal teacher–student interaction play a key role in this lesson?
10. How do you think Mr. Servon was assessing the students as the lesson progressed?

# 6

# FRACTIONS

## What's It All About?

**The Activity**

**Focus: Mr. Thayer uses linear fraction models to have students compare fractions.**

As the students put away their maps from the social studies lesson, Mr. Thayer distributed a sheet (see first diagram on next page).

He placed an acetate copy of the sheet on the overhead projector. He said, "I want you to turn the sheet so the large rectangle is at the top. You can see how I have set it up on the overhead projector. Then I want you to write the numeral 1 in the middle of the largest rectangle. Sarah, after you do that on your sheet, please go up and write the numeral 1 on the overhead sheet (see second diagram on next page). This tells us that the bar is the unit that we will use for our work." He continued to move around the room to help students who did not understand.

"Now, with your partner, take a minute and discuss what each of the boxes in the next row would equal if the top box is 1 unit or 1 whole." He gave the students time to discuss this and began to hear students talking about 1 half. Finally, he asked, "Maria, how much is each box worth?"

"One half," Maria said. "Great," he replied. "Now, be careful because we are going to treat one half differently than you may have done in other grades. We know that each of the boxes right under the 1-box is worth one half. So, I want you to write the word *half* in each of the two boxes. Do not write *one half*, just the word *half*. Letitia, fill in the pieces on the overhead sheet."

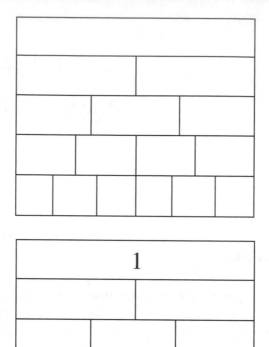

"Why don't we write 'one half'?" asked Rodney, "it is only one." "Good question. Stop your work and listen to Rodney. Rodney, repeat your question." After Rodney did so, Mr. Thayer held up a board eraser. He said, "If we were to label this with the word *eraser*, would we put a *one* in front of the word *eraser*?" "No," came the call from the class. "So, that is the way we are going to look at this part of the unit. It is a thing called 'half,' and for now, not a number."

After the students wrote "half" in each box, Mr. Thayer said, "Work with each other and look at each of the other boxes as parts of the unit. Then, decide what word you should write in the other boxes. You have four minutes. Remember, what word should you write? GO!!!"

Amid the chatter, Mr. Thayer walked around the room. As he saw a group of students filling in the rest of the chart correctly, he asked

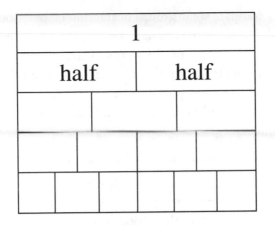

one member of the group to fill in the thirds, the fourths, and then the sixths on the overhead projector. At the end of four minutes, the chart on the overhead was completed.

"Anyone get caught putting 'fifth' in the last set of boxes? Be careful. There are six boxes which means that each box is a 'sixth'." Mr. Thayer then distributed a pair of scissors to each student. "Now, before we go any farther, cut up the chart into individual fraction pieces. Let's take four minutes to do that." As the students began the cutting, Mr. Thayer took the acetate off the overhead and replaced it with pieces which he had cut during his planning period. When the students were done, he continued.

| 1 | | | | | |
|---|---|---|---|---|---|
| half | | | half | | |
| third | | third | | third | |
| fourth | | fourth | | fourth | fourth |
| sixth | sixth | sixth | sixth | sixth | sixth |

"Now let's compare some groups of fraction pieces. Look up here to the overhead. If I want to compare the fraction made up of '2 thirds' and the fraction made up of '2 fourths,' I make a 'train' out of each of them and set the trains parallel to each other from the same starting point. Then I can compare the trains like this." As the students watched, Mr. Thayer placed a train of 2 thirds alongside a train of 2 fourths as shown.

| third | third |
|-------|-------|
| fourth | fourth |

"So you can see that 2 thirds are larger than 2 fourths. Now work with your groups to compare 2 fourths and 1 half." As the students worked in their groups, Mr. Thayer again walked through the class to give assistance and listen to the students' discussions.

"Amy, show us on the overhead what you did and give us your

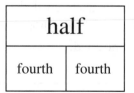

| half | |
|------|------|
| fourth | fourth |

answer." Amy moved to the overhead and placed the pieces as shown.

Amy said, "I made a train using 1 half and then with 2 fourths. I set them together and the train of 2 fourths was equal to the train of 1 half. So, 2 fourths are equal to one half."

"Great," said Mr. Thayer. "Now one last question: Compare 1 half and 3 fourths. Take two minutes." In a short period of time, Myrna raised her hand. "Myrna?" said Mr. Thayer.

"But couldn't you tell that 3 fourths is larger since you only need 2 fourths to equal one half?" "I want everyone to discuss Myrna's explanation with their partner and then write out the explanation in their journals. Explain it once more Myrna." After Myrna gave her reasoning again, the groups went to work. "Can we use diagrams?" asked Ken. "Yes, you can always use diagrams in your explanation."

"Now I'm going to give each of you an envelope to put your fraction pieces in. Also copy this question from the chart paper for homework. It is pretty much what Myrna said."

---

### Thinking about Math

If you know that 2 fourths equals 1 half, then you know that 3 fourths is greater than 1 half. Use diagrams to help to make this idea clear.

---

"When you finish with these, take out your social studies maps and look at some of the places we discussed yesterday and make a list of the countries they are in."

## The Mathematics

Fractions are relative. That is, 1 half is not always the same size. This concept is different from whole numbers. When I compare 10 trucks to 10 straws, although the trucks may be larger, I can match the trucks and straws in a one-to-one fashion. Not so with fractions. If my unit is as wide as this page, 1 half would be much larger than the 1 half the students used in the activity. So, in dealing with fractions, one of the first ideas that students must focus on is the unit for the comparisons. Also, in our language, we must be careful not to state that "1 half is always larger than 1 fourth" since this is not always true. Sometimes in our zeal to use the language of understanding (chapter 1) there can be misinformation.

The concept of fractions is developed here using the idea of the quantitative adjective and the quantitative noun. For example, with the fraction 2 thirds, 2 describes how many thirds there are. So, 2 (which we call the numerator) is an adjective telling the number of things and thirds (which we call the denominator) tells us (or denotes) the name of the fraction piece that we have. This is the same type of mathematical grammar that we saw with multiplication in chapter 4.

These are used to keep in the students' view the idea that the denominator of a fraction is not a number as they know it from whole numbers but the name of a part of a unit. In this way, when it comes to operations, it will help them to remember that they must only add like things (like thirds and thirds) and they cannot simply add unlike things (like fourths and halves) even if there are numerals in the denominator.

This system also presents to students the inverse nature of fractions. That is, the higher the number-name in the denominator, the more pieces are made from the unit and therefore, the smaller the pieces. This idea, which can be called "inverse proportional thinking" is one that depends on the cognitive maturity of the student and can truly be addressed only when the curriculum creators know that children are cognitively mature enough to understand it.

The concept of comparison of fractions contains both equivalence and inequality (greater than/less than.) As a result, both are contained in the same lesson since the visuals generate the understanding. From this, the procedures can be understood. For example when the students see that 2 fourths are equivalent to 1 half, the teacher can use this to address the formal procedure and discuss why a factor of 2 plays a prominent role in the symbolic representation (2 fourths has twice as many pieces as 1 half).

Just to say, "Since, in ¾ both the numerator and denominator have a common factor of 2, I can divide both of them by 2 and establish an equivalent fraction ½" gives the students nothing but a procedure with an accompanying lack of understanding, which creates difficulties later on in their mathematical development.

## The Plan

**Title**: Introducing fractional concepts

**Teacher Objective**: Introduce the concept of fractions; introduce equivalent fractions; use pieces to have students compare fractions.

**Objective for Students**: Using models, you will compare sizes of fractions.

**NCTM Focal Points 3–5**: Number and operations: Use models, benchmarks, and equivalent forms to judge the size of fractions.

**Materials**: Fraction template (see Appendix B), scissors, overhead transparency of fraction template, legal size envelopes, questions for homework on chart paper.

*Thinking about Math*

If you know that 2 fourths equals 1 half, then you know that 3 fourths is greater than 1 half. Use diagrams to help to make this idea clear.

*Beginning Stage*

1. Distribute the fraction model to students.
2. Explain that the large rectangle should be at the top of the page.
3. Have the students write "1" in the middle of the first rectangle.

*Middle Stage*

4. Have student pairs discuss the two rectangles (boxes) under the one marked "1."
5. When you tell the students to write the word *half* be ready to answer questions: "Why do we not write one half?" "Why don't we write one over two?"
6. After writing "half," choose Letitia to write the names on the overhead.
7. Continue to have students name the parts of the fractions on the template.

8. When completed, have students cut up pieces.

*Final Stage*

9. Have the students discuss these problems: Compare 2 thirds and 2 fourths, 1 half and 2 fourths. At the end of class, have students place fraction pieces in their envelopes and also copy down the homework. Call their attention to the homework.

## Putting It All Together

As you may know from your own experience, fractions can be a confusing concept for students, which can lead to difficulty throughout their school careers. This lesson shows the students the visual/linguistic characteristics of fractions; that is, using diagrams and their background in literacy to explain the numerator/denominator relationship.

Many times, students see both the numerator and denominator as numbers. As a result, the addition of ½ + ⅓ erroneously equals ⅖. (Since they just see the denominators as numbers, the students add them. What could be easier? Or more incorrect???)

As a teacher, you must lay the foundation so that as students move along in mathematics they can fall back to original meanings and descriptions to reconstruct their knowledge if they become confused in a situation.

In the next two lessons, we will address two of the more difficult ideas in operations with fractions, addition of fractions which have unlike denominators and the division of fractions (You know, the old "invert and multiply" routine!) Again the visual/linguistic modeling will help students draw out the meaning and allow them to see the rationale and reasoning behind the procedures they need to learn.

## Doing Some Mathematics

Because fractions tend not to be the favorite of a lot of people, students and teachers alike, I would like to give you some exercises to do. The rule is "Use the Fraction Pieces!!"

While you are doing these, think about how you could write it out as a procedure for your students (moving them through the connecting level as explained in chapter 1). And, if you come up with something that is not the "standard" procedure, ask yourself, "Would this be more understandable for my students?" If it would be, then students will benefit from your work.

For each fraction name at least one fraction of the same size which has a different name.

    a. 2 fourths           b. 1 third           c. 2 thirds

For each pair of fractions, find the fraction which is larger.

    d. 1 third and 3 fourths      e. 3 fourths and 5 sixths
    f. 2 thirds and 5 sixths
    g. Explain this: For example "c," you should have 4 sixths as a fraction equivalent to 2 thirds. How can this help you answer example f without using the pieces?

## Reflections

*Reflecting on the Activity*

1. Mr. Thayer could have completed the chart on the overhead himself. Why did he not do this?
2. In the Activity, how do the physical models overcome difficulties students may have?
3. How did the language of mathematics develop in the lesson?

*Reflecting on the Mathematics*

4. Explain in simple nonmathematical terms what a denominator represents.
5. Why is clarity in the use of language important in dealing with fractions?

*Reflecting on the Plan*

6. Why did Mr. Thayer plan to have the students cut out all the pieces after they were set up on the sheet?
7. How did Mr. Thayer use writing to enhance the learning experience?
8. Did he give the students a very complicated idea to write about?

*Your Reflections*

9. Why do people (including students) have difficulty with fractions?
10. Write down why you have trouble with fractions. Have three or four of your classmates do the same. Then, put these papers without your names in a bag and take one and read it. Have the group discuss the difficulty. (Putting them in a bag and taking one keeps a level of anonymity which should make all feel comfortable.)
11. Do you see the physical models causing any difficulties in the learning of fractions?

# 7

# FRACTIONS

## Adding Unlike Things? Impossible!

**The Activity**

**Focus: Through the use of linear fraction models, Ms. Berg uses problem solving to introduce students to adding fractions having unlike denominators.**

As the students put away their books from a previous class, Ms. Berg uncovered a problem on the flip chart.

> Rodney completed 40 miles of his trip on Monday and 25 miles of his trip on Tuesday. What total of his trip did he complete in the two days? How did you arrive at your answer?

"Work in your groups to solve this problem and draw a diagram which will be a model for what we will do today. Take about two minutes. Go." Ms. Berg moved about the classroom as the students worked on the problem. It was obvious that all the students had a correct answer.

"Abby, what did your group say?" Abby reported, "He went 65 miles. We added 40 miles and 25 miles."

"Good," said Ms. Berg. She then asked them to take out the fraction pieces and sort them out on the tables. (From previous classes, each student had constructed two sets of fraction pieces.) "Now apply that solution model to this problem." Again, she flipped the chart paper to reveal a problem.

> Cynthia completed ½ of her trip on Monday and ⅓ of her trip on Tuesday. Use your fraction pieces to find out what part of the total trip she completed in the two days? How did you arrive at your answer?

"This time, I am going to give you three minutes to solve it. Go."

As she moved about the room, she received several looks from the students. One student asked, "Is ½ and ⅓ a good answer, Ms. Berg?"

"No, Freddie," she said, "It does not give me the total. It just restates the parts of the situation. Boys and girls," she said, "use your fraction pieces."

With this, students began to make a train using a half piece and a third piece. Michelle raised her hand. "Yes, Michelle," said Ms. Berg. "You keep saying that we can only add things that are alike. But one half and one third are two different things. How can we add them?"

Ms. Berg called the class to attention and asked Michelle to repeat her question. When she did, Ms. Berg said, "Anyone have an idea?" Jeff said, "Is this like we did the other day with making fractions of one type into another?" "Want to explain that in a little more detail, Jeff?" said Ms. Berg. Jeff continued, "Well, we worked on fractions like one half and made it into fourths and sixths. With thirds, we made them into sixths. So, could we do something like that?" "You could," said Ms. Berg, "and now, back to work."

As she moved about the room, she "wandered" over to Jeff's group and heard someone say, "But if we get other pieces to equal them, then we can add the other pieces." After some moving around of the pieces, the group began to put sixths together. Before they could look at Ms. Berg for confirmation, she moved away.

Finally, Ms. Berg called the class back to a full group and asked for ideas. Sadie said, "We changed the one half and one third to sixths. Then since these were the same name we could add them."

"Sadie, go to the overhead and show us what you mean," said Ms. Berg. Sadie went to the overhead and using the overhead pieces showed that 1 half was equal to 3 sixths and 1 third was equal to 2 sixths.

| half | | | third | |
|---|---|---|---|---|
| sixth | sixth | sixth | sixth | sixth |

She continued, "So, now that we have the same type of fraction, we can add them. So the answer is 5 sixths." "So what is the solution to the problem, Jeff?" "Cynthia completed 5 sixths of her trip in the two days."

"Very good. Now in your groups, I want you to go around the table and each person at the table will explain this solution to the others. This is just to make sure everyone knows what is going on. If someone has difficulty with it, I expect the others in the group to help. You can use your pieces as part of your explanation. Then, after you do that, I want you to work on a solution to the problem on the chart."

She flipped the chart paper and showed:

How much of her trip did Cynthia still have to go? Explain your answer.

As Ms. Berg moved about the room, she heard students explaining in their own words how the problem was solved. She then began to hear solutions to the last problem.

In a few minutes, she called, "Okay, how long does she still have to go, Allan?"

"She still has one sixth of the trip left. We know that on Monday and Tuesday she finished five sixths of her trip. So, for the complete trip, she needs only one more sixth."

Ms. Berg asked, "And when she completes that one more sixth, how much of the trip has she made, Arlene?" "The whole trip." "Or?" "6 sixths."

"Good, so today we learned another application of the idea that you can only add things which are the same, to fractions. We'll continue this tomorrow. For homework, I want you once again to explain how you put 1 half and 1 third together. So, let's put away our fraction pieces and get ready to go to music."

## The Mathematics

Mention fractions to many students, and there is a grimace. For some reason (we'll discuss this below), students neither like nor understand fractions. However, they are not the only people. Put about 30 adults together and it would be interesting to see their reaction to fractions.

For an education group, this could include elementary teachers (like yourself) but also history teachers, English teachers, and others.

Yes, many adults do not like fractions either. And the next generation of adults who do not like fractions is moving through the grades as you read this. And you are one of the people who can help to break this trend.

But the big question is, "What is it about fractions that makes them so unlikable?" Well, first, most people never understood them from the beginning. They learned them in an instructional model which gave them the procedures and they were told that they would understand it later (a "later" which never arrived.) Some, like the students in your present class, remembered the procedures and passed the tests. But how many did neither? Those students are also moving through the grades as you read this.

From a mathematical view, fractions are not as definitive as whole numbers. Similar to what was said in chapter 6, we know what four of something looks like. There are four of them. I can see them in my mind if they are too big (4 planets is a good example). However, when we talk about 2 thirds, things get, well, messy. And when we begin to discuss the idea that 1 third can added to 1 half and we get sixths for a sum, it seems to go against the grain.

With whole numbers, when we add things, they must be the same. 2 trucks added to 3 cars cannot give us an answer of cars or trucks. UNLESS we decide to talk about vehicles. Then 2 trucks can be designated as 2 vehicles while 3 cars can be designated as 3 vehicles. Then, we have 5 vehicles.

So, like whole numbers, with fractions we can actually talk about adding two things which are not alike and we do so by equating each of the fractions to something else, kind of a third party (Is that a pun?)

In the Activity, the students were asked to add 1 half and 1 third. But, they know they cannot because these quantities represent different quantitative nouns (half and third). Yet, through the "magic" of equivalent fractions, they can find representatives of each fraction which have the same quantitative noun, namely sixths. So, 1 half and 1 third become 3 sixths and 2 sixths respectively for a sum of 5 sixths.

In a sense, halves, thirds, and sixths set up a "family" of denominators just like 2, 3, and 6 set up a family of facts when you deal with multiplication and division. Since 2, 5, and 10 set up a family of facts with multiplication and division, what do you think the family of denominators is? So, when you have to add 1 half and 3 fifths, what quantitative noun do you think will help?

From here, you as the teacher need to begin to lead students to the written algorithm which has students show that $\frac{1}{2} = \frac{3}{6}$ and $\frac{1}{3} = \frac{2}{6}$ and how they are added together, that $\frac{3}{6} + \frac{2}{6} = \frac{5}{6}$ and why you do not add the '6's'. (Remember, they represent quantitative nouns, not quantitative adjectives.)

## The Plan

*Lesson Plan*

**Teacher Objective**: Students will be able to add two fractions with unlike denominators.

**Objective for Students**: Applying "You only add the same things" to adding fractions.

**NCTM Focal Points 3–5**: Understand the meanings and effects of arithmetic operations with fractions.

**Materials**: Two sets of fraction pieces for each student. On chart paper, write two problems to be used in the session.

Problem 1: Rodney completed 40 miles of his trip on Monday and 25 miles of his trip on Tuesday. What total of his trip did he complete in the two days? How did you arrive at your answer?

Problem 2: Cynthia completed ½ of her trip on Monday and ⅓ of her trip on Tuesday. Use your fraction pieces to find out what part of the total trip she completed in the two days? How did you arrive at your answer?

Problem 3: How much of her trip did Cynthia still have to go? Explain your answer.

*Beginning Stage*

1. Explain to the students that you wish them to solve a problem about someone taking a trip. Tell them to work in their groups. Uncover Problem 1 on the chart paper.
2. Give students two minutes to find a solution. When they are done, review the solution and its structure, the idea that they are adding to find the part of the trip completed.

*Middle Stage*

3. Ask students to take out their fraction pieces and sort them on the desks.
4. Give the students Problem 2 to solve in their groups. Encourage students to use their fraction pieces. Move about the room to listen to discussions.
5. Call class to order and have a student explain the answer using the overhead pieces.
6. Have each student explain the answer to their group to insure that all can do it.

*Final Stage*

7. Ask students to go into their groups and decide how much of the trip Cynthia still has to travel.
8. Give the groups two minutes to solve.
9. Move through the room to listen to groups. Have each group recorder write the explanation on the board.
10. In the following discussion, reinforce the idea that the entire trip is 6 sixths.
11. Have students copy down each of the different explanations.
12. *Homework:* Have students read the different explanations and be ready to discuss them tomorrow.

## Doing Some Mathematics

Make three sets of fraction pieces. Use the template in Appendix B. Then complete these exercises using the fraction pieces. Remember two ideas as you work these problems. When you have enough fraction pieces to equal 1 (such as 4 fourths) trade them for a 1 bar. Also, when you have a fraction, make sure it is in its simplest form (least number of pieces). For example, 3 sixths can be exchanged for 1 half.

1. 1 half + 1 fourth
2. 1 sixth + 1 third
3. 1 half + 2 thirds
4. 1 half + 3 fourths
5. 5 sixths + 2 thirds
6. 1 and 2 thirds + 1 half
7. If you were to add 1 fourth and 1 third, what kind of pieces would you need to create an answer?

## Putting It All Together

When adding fractions, we use the same concept that is used in all addition, namely, you can only add things that are the same. In algebra, we cannot add x and $x^2$ because they are not the same thing. They even sound different when you say them.

However, there is an added concept when dealing with fractions with unlike denominators, which is the idea of looking for some type of similarity. For example, if you have 3 2-dollar bills (they are out there) and 4 5-dollar bills, you cannot have a total amount by simply adding 3 and 4. The bills we are using are not same. However, we do have the system of changing them into 1 dollar bills and then finding the total.

So also with fractions: As seen in the Activity and in Doing Some Mathematics, what is being added (half, third, etc.) is not the same (they are not called by the same quantitative noun). Therefore, we cannot add them as they initially appear. The materials stop students from moving onward where they simply add the numerators and then add the denominators to find a total. With fraction pieces, 1 half added to 1 third cannot possibly equal 2 fifths. It just does not make sense. However, when using the written symbols, if students lack understanding of what the parts of the fraction mean, especially the meaning of the denominator, they have no way of seeing the process as just adding anything that is there.

For the learning process, this means that pure symbolic references will not make the case with many students. They need to "see" and "touch" what is happening so that correct processes can be reconstructed as they move on to other ideas in mathematics.

**NOTE:** Sometimes you will hear that ratios can be written as fractions. That is true but that does not make them the same, especially when it comes to operations. For example, if a softball player comes to bat 2 times and gets 1 hit, the ratio of hits to times at bat is 1 to 2 or ½. If in the next game, she comes to bat 3 times and again gets 1 hit, the ratio of hits to times at bat is 1 to 3 or ⅓. Now, when we look at both games, she went to bat 5 times and got 2 hits. The ratio of hits to times at bat is 2 to 5 or ⅖. That is actually the sum of ½ and ⅓ when they stand for ratios. But be careful. Many elementary students have not had enough experience to realize these kinds of contextual differences when they see numbers written in the same way.

## Reflections

*Reflecting on the Activity*

1. How did Ms. Berg have the children learn the difference between numerators and denominators?
2. In which part of the activity should Ms. Berg be very careful that the students do not become confused as to what they could do?

*Reflecting on the Mathematics*

3. What role do the ideas of quantitative noun and quantitative adjective play in addition of fractions with unlike denominators?
4. How are denominators used in adding fractions with unlike denominators linked to multiplication and division facts?
5. Why must fractions have the equal denominators before you add?

*Reflecting on the Plan*

6. What do you think is an important thing that the teacher does before the lesson to ensure that there are no gaps in the learning process?
7. What do students need to know before they are ready for this lesson?
8. What type of classroom management is used in many of the Activities you have read about so far in this book?

*Your Reflections*

9. From your own experience, what is the difficulty that students have in dealing with adding fractions with unlike denominators?
10. What would be a way of explaining to students why you cannot add ½ and ⅓ unless you make some changes to the denominator?
11. What confusion can arise if a teacher uses the term *Adding unlike fractions*?

# 8

# FRACTIONS

## Dividing into Small Pieces?

**The Activity**

**Focus: Ms. Teadle uses the fraction models to have students understand the meaning of division of fractions, how this concept fits into the overall idea of division, and what the procedure "flip the second fraction and multiply" really means.**

Ms. Teadle placed a set of fraction pieces on the overhead projector. When students were settled, she said, "We have worked with division as a sharing process. We are now going to try to use that idea to see what occurs with fractions. So, take out your fraction pieces and sort them out on your desk. I have done this with the fraction pieces on the overhead." While the students did this, Ms. Teadle turned on the overhead projector to show one of the arrangements possible and then moved about the room to insure students were not having difficulties with this.

"Now in your groups, I want you to take 2 ones and make a train out of them." She gave the students a moment to set this up. "Now, make another train using enough thirds to equal a train of ones. When you are done, draw this as a diagram in your notebooks."

While students in the groups did this, Ms. Teadle arranged 2 ones as a train on the overhead and then moved about the room. At one point, she asked Sandra to go to the overhead and show what she had done. Sandra walked to the overhead and arranged the pieces.

"Everyone look at the screen and check your work with Sandra's." After a minute or so, Ms. Teadle said, "In your notebooks below the

| 1 | | | 1 | | |
|---|---|---|---|---|---|
| third | third | third | third | third | third |

diagram, write an equation for what your diagram tells you." Jeffrey said, "This just means that 2 ones is equal to 6 thirds. But we knew that already." "Correct," said Ms. Teadle. She gave them a minute or so to write what Jeffrey had said.

"Now let's look at the statement that I have written on the chart paper. I want you to discuss an answer in your groups." Ms. Teadle uncovered a statement on the chart paper. It read:

"When I divide 2 ones by 1 third, what do I get for an answer?"

"Okay," she said, "you have three minutes to discuss this in your groups and decide what the question is asking and what it means to divide by one third." Ms. Teadle moved about the room to listen to the various discussions and to insure that students stayed on task. As time ran out, she asked the recorder in each group to write the response on the board.

What everyone saw on the board was the idea that you want to find how many thirds fit into 2 ones."

"So," said Ms. Teadle, "if we divide 2 ones by 1 third, we break each one into 3 thirds and we get a total of 6 thirds." "So, here's the problem," Ms. Teadle said and wrote "2 ÷ ⅓ = " on the chalkboard.

"Now, from what we have done, here today, what is the answer and how would you get it?" The groups worked for a few minutes and then Joni raised her hand. Joni said, "Multiply by 3." "Why?" "Because you have 2 sets of 3 thirds."

"So what do you write?" "2 × 3"

Ms. Teadle continued to write and now had: 2 ÷ ⅓ = 2 × 3 =

And the answer?" "6." She finished writing: 2 ÷ ⅓ = 2 × 3 = 6.

"One last question. What is the label of the number 6? What do you have 6 of?"

Marcus raised his hand. "We have 6 thirds." "Good," said Ms. Teadle, "because our model does not show us 6 but 6 thirds."

"Now," said Ms. Teadle, "Work in your groups and decide on a general rule for dividing by unit fractions, such as ¼, and ⅕. Then, explain why. You have two minutes." In about a minute, all the groups were done and Ms. Teadle called them to order.

"Reggie, explain what your group decided." Reggie said, "When you divide by a unit fraction, you multiply by the denominator of the unit fraction. You do this because each of your ones is broken into that many pieces. So, seven divided by one fifth would equal 35 because each of the 7 ones is broken into five fifths."

"Great. Now for homework, here are some exercises I want you to do. Also, the last question asks you to explain what is happening." "You mean like Reggie just said, Ms. Teadle," said Samantha. "Well yes, but if you want to say it in your own way, you can."

## The Mathematics

As was discussed in chapter 5, division has two interpretations. There is the sharing model which was used with whole numbers in chapter 5 and the 'how many can be found in' which is what is used here. Dividing 3 by ½ means "How many ½'s can be found in 3?" Since each one contains 2 halves, 3 ones would contain 6 halves: so, $3 \div \frac{1}{2} = 6$. (For some reason, the label on the 6 which is "halves" is usually left out.)

What this means is that the number of halves in any number is equal to twice the value of the number. This is the reason for the age old rule of "invert and multiply."

Now, when you divide 3 by ⅔, there is another part. When you divide by ⅔, in a sense you are trying to find how many "pairs of thirds" there are. So, dividing by ⅔ means that you multiply the quantity by 3 to find the number of thirds, and then divide that number by 2 to get the number of "pairs of thirds." (Remember that a pair of 1-thirds is also called 2 thirds. Use your fraction pieces to find 2 divided by ⅔. Compare your answer to the "invert and multiply" method.)

The number of 2-thirds in a quantity is half the number of 1-thirds in the quantity. It is "strange" that there are more 1-thirds than 2-thirds. For example, with 6 ones, $6 \div \frac{1}{3} = 18$ and $6 \div \frac{2}{3} = 9$.) This is somewhat different from what students may believe since, with whole numbers, 2 of something is usually more than 1 of something. Again, there is a difference between whole numbers and fractions.

So, $4 \div \frac{2}{3}$ means you first find that there are 12 thirds in 4 and then divide by 2 to find how many sets of 2-thirds (or pairs of thirds) there are in 12. From this you can see that to find $4 \div \frac{2}{3}$, you begin with 4 × $\frac{3}{2}$ which shows that you will multiply by 3 to find the number of thirds in 4 and then divide by 2 to find the number of "pairs of thirds" (namely the number of 2-thirds in 4). From this comes the idea of why you invert and multiply.

I know this sounds very tricky and may leave you tongue-tied. However, read it over while you complete the work with the *fraction pieces* and it will become clearer and make it easier for you to discuss it with your students as long as they have their fraction pieces.

## The Plan

**Title**: Introducing dividing by a fraction.

**Teacher Objective**: Students will understand how to apply the concept of division to fractions. Students will know how to divide a whole number by a fraction.

**Objective for Students**: We will break whole quantities into the same fractional part.

**NCTM Focal Points 3–5**: Understand the meanings and effects of arithmetic operations with fractions.

**Materials**: Fraction pieces.

**Statement on chart**: "When I divide 2 ones by 1 third, what do I get for an answer?"

**Homework**: Divide 3 by ½ Divide 5 by ¼ Divide 10 by ½.

Explain what happens when you divide a whole number by a unit fraction.

*Beginning Stage*

1. Have students use their fraction pieces to decide how many thirds are needed when dividing 2 into third pieces.

*Middle Stage*

2. When done, introduce the concept with statement on chart.
3. Have students develop a rule for dividing fractions.
4. Use this discussion to develop the equation: $2 \div \frac{1}{3} = 2 \times 3 = 6$ in two parts:
   a. $2 \div \frac{1}{3}$ = to state what we are looking for.
   b. $2 \div \frac{1}{3} = 2 \times 3$ to show symbolically what the students do with their fraction pieces.
   d. $2 \div \frac{1}{3} = 2 \times 3 = 6$ to establish an answer.
5. Have students discuss the label for 6 and how it relates to the activity.

*Final Stage*

6. Have students practice with 2 divided by ¼ and 2 divided by ⅕ to have them transfer the ideas to a totally symbolic communication.

## Doing Some Mathematics

Use fraction pieces to solve the following. For each exercise, rewrite the example to explain what it is really saying. Also, write the answer in a complete sentence.

1. 2 ÷ fourth
2. 1 ÷ 1-sixth
3. 2 ÷ 1-sixth
4. 4 ÷ 2-thirds
5. 8 ÷ 2-thirds
6. 3 ÷ 1 and 1-half

## Putting It All Together

From a teaching/learning perspective, the important ideas seen here are to show students that division of fractions is similar in concept to division with whole numbers and why one multiplies to find the answer. The fraction pieces make this abundantly clear. The idea that you are taking a number of things (units) and breaking them into fraction pieces means that the number of fraction pieces in the end is going to be more than the number of units you began with.

Although, you must remember that the quantity at the beginning and the quantity at the end of the problem are equal. The parts of the quantity have just been rearranged.

In having students learn this, it is necessary for them to see the effect of dividing a quantity into fractional pieces and the number of pieces increasing. As seen in the Activity, the visual is extremely important as is the need for the students to actually do the "dividing."

## Reflections

*Reflecting on the Activity*

1. What did Ms. Teadle use to have the students check their work? How effective do you think this is?
2. How did Ms. Teadle keep the discussion in a language of understanding mode (chapter 1) throughout the lesson?

*Reflecting on the Mathematics*

3. Explain why students may have difficulty with the concepts and skills involved in dividing fractions.
4. Why do you multiply by 3 when you are dividing by 1-third?
5. Explain how division of whole numbers and division by a fraction are similar.
6. If a student were to ask, "Is this true for fractions like 1-seventh?" what would you do?

*Reflecting on the Plan*

7. What was the most important idea for Ms. Teadle to keep in mind during the planning?
8. Why do you think she decided to include "2 divided by $\frac{1}{5}$" in the lesson?

*Your Reflection*

9. Why do you think dividing by a fraction is difficult?

10. If a student asks, "Why, when you are dividing by small fractions you sometimes get a large answer?" how do you give them a good reason for this?

# 9

# DECIMALS

## Operations Before Rules

**The Activity**

**Focus: Mr. Gardner uses a collection of rainfall data to introduce addition and subtraction of decimals.**

In science, Mr. Gardner's class has been discussing the ecology of water with the study of droughts and floods. Mr. Gardner asked the students to choose a city on each continent and then use the Internet to find the rainfall in the months May through August in each of the cities. He chose two of them, Paris and Beijing, for this mathematics activity.

As class began, Mr. Gardner distributed the data sheet of rain for Paris and Beijing. He also placed a transparency copy on the overhead projector (see chart on next page).

"Let's do some estimating. I want you to estimate the total amount of rain in Paris for June, July, and August. I'll give you five minutes to do this." As the students worked, Mr. Gardner moved about the room assisting where students needed it.

As the time ended, he said, "Melanie, can you show us what you did?" Melanie came to the overhead and explained as she wrote: "I rounded 30.05 to 30, 23.68 to 24 and 19.29 to 20. Then I added 30, 24, and 20 and got 74."

| Cities | May | June | July | August |
|--------|-----|------|------|--------|
| Beijing | 3.3 cm | 7.8 cm | 22.4 cm | 17 cm |
| Paris | 32.3 cm | 30.05 cm | 23.68 cm | 19.29 cm |

As she spoke, Melanie wrote on the overhead:

$$32.3 \rightarrow 32$$
$$30.05 \rightarrow 30$$
$$23.68 \rightarrow \underline{24}$$
$$86$$

"And answering in a complete sentence?" asked Mr. Gardner. "The estimate of rain was 86 centimeters."

"Good," said Mr. Gardner. "Now, let's look at how we could get an actual total."

"How about just using a calculator?" asked Gabriella.

"Well that will give you the answer. But it will not show you how it is related to the rest of mathematics. And that is also important. So let's get started."

With that, Mr. Gardner asked Mark to go to the overhead projector. "I want everyone to watch Mark's work. First, Mark, write down the whole numbers in the rain totals for Paris for June, July, and August."

Mark wrote:

$$32$$
$$30$$
$$23$$

"Now, complete each number with the decimal."
Mark wrote:

$$32.3$$
$$30.05$$
$$23.68$$

To the class, Mr. Gardner said, "Write down each of the place values you see in this addition."

After a short time, he called on Mei. "I have tens, ones, tenths, and hundredths."

Mr. Gardner said, "Now I want everyone to copy what Mark wrote and add the place values that Mei said."

"But there are no hundredths in the first number," said Teri.

"So, when we do not have any of a certain place, what do we write, Teri?"

"Zero," said Teri.

"Do we have to put in a zero," asked Staci.

"No," said Mr. Gardner, "It is up to you."

Finally, he asked Mark to put the total, 86.03, and had the students check their work.

"Leslie, could you tell us how to add numbers that have decimal places?"

Leslie said, "You add the place values that are the same, like tens to tens, tenths to tenth. Like that." "Good. Now, everyone, in your notebooks write a heading: 'Rule for adding decimals.' and then write the rule."

When they were done with this, Mr. Gardner called the students' attention to the chart paper. "Here is a homework problem for you to do. So go ahead and finish up."

**Homework:** Estimate the difference in rainfall in June between Beijing and Paris. Find the total for all the months in Paris and Beijing.

## The Mathematics

In our discussion here, the term *decimal number* will refer to a number which is represented by numerals on both sides of the decimal point, such as 36.737 which is what people normally refer to when they use the term *decimal number*.

Now, with decimals, as with other topics in mathematics, instruction tends to have students remember rules without rationale. Actually, when teachers tell children that decimals are just like whole numbers except for some rules on how to place the decimal point, they are not focusing on the correct aspect of the number, the place values involved.

In addition of decimals, as with whole numbers, we can only add like things or like place values. Just as we add tens to tens and thousands to thousands, so also we can only add tenths to tenths and hundredths to hundredths. The decimal point simple separates the part of the number that is greater than or equal to 1 from the part of the number that is less than 1 (if you are using a decimal point, see note below for an explanation of this).

If after many uses students begin to see the pattern that the decimal point in the sum always falls underneath the decimals in the addends, it can be discussed by understanding the context in which it is occurring.

It is easy to see (sounds like "clearly from the above" as you find in many mathematics textbooks) how similar ideas can be applied to subtraction.

In order to see the pattern for multiplication of decimals, initial instruction should focus on the placement of the decimal after the estimation of the whole numbers. Let's use 3.4 × 2.7 as an example. Most students know the procedure for multiplying 34 × 27. So let's use that to move to multiplication with decimals. With a very rough estimate, we know that our answer is going to be about 6 since the product of the whole numbers, 3 × 2 is equal to 6. Now, let's just multiply 34 × 27. Notice that there are no decimals. The product here is 918.

Now we need to place the decimal. There are four options: 0.918; 9.18; 91.8; 918.

However, our estimate is 6. So which of these options gives us a product close to our estimate? Obviously it is 9.18.

Division of a decimal by a whole number entails the sharing aspects of division as we saw in chapter 5. When we divide 18.6 by 3, we share out the 18 three ways so each receives 6 and then we share out 6 tenths with each receiving 2 tenths. So, the answer is that each would receive 6 and 2 tenths or 6.2.

For those of you who are wondering about dividing by a decimal (56 divided by 3.2) you should see a wonderful use of the calculator here. Although there is nothing wrong with doing such an example with paper and pencil, for this students need to understand why the "movement of the decimal" rule works. They need to understand first that 56 divided by 3.2 yields the same quotient as 560 divided by 32 or 5,600 divided by 320. However, this for immature number theorists can be quite overwhelming. So, we can begin to use a calculator to compute with such divisions.

So, to generalize, in the teaching of addition, multiplication, and subtraction of decimals, estimation plays an essential role in laying the foundation from which students can find and understand the traditional decimals operations "rules." In their doing this, they can use the mathematical concept that only numbers in the same place value can be added and/or subtracted.

### The Plan

**Topic**: Adding decimal numbers.
**Teacher Objective**: Students will learn how to add decimals.
**Objective for Students**: Investigate total rainfall in some of the cities that you previously investigated.
**NCTM Focal Points 3–5**: Understand the meanings and effects of arithmetic operations with decimals.
**Materials**: Data sheet of rainfall in Beijing and Paris:
    Chart paper with:
        Find the total for all the months in Paris and Beijing.
        Homework: Estimate the difference in rainfall in June between Beijing and Paris.

*Beginning Stage*

1. Distribute data sheet of rainfall. Ask students to estimate the difference for the two cities in the month of June.

*Middle Stage*

2. Choose a student to go to the overhead and show how the estimate was done.

3. Have a student go to the overhead and give her or him the steps to use subtraction to find the exact answer.
   a. Write out the whole number part of each number.
   b. Complete each number.
   c. Subtract the place values.

*Final Stage*

4. Review concepts and procedure for adding decimals (estimating and adding numbers having the same place value).
5. *Homework:* Find the total rainfall for all 12 months in both Paris and Beijing.
   Estimate the difference in rainfall in June between Beijing and Paris.

## Doing Some Mathematics

Use the idea of this chapter to find: (1) An estimate for the answer; (2) the actual answer to each of the following.

a. 0.67 + 8.94 + 12.3         d.  3.4 × 8.6
b. 46.2 – 5.92                e.  1.2 × 12.6
c. 5.67 – 0.89                f.  12.8 ÷ 4
g. Explain why 3.4 × 0.8 would not have an estimate of 3 × 0 = 0.

## Putting It All Together

When dealing with operations of addition, subtraction, multiplication, and division, numbers which include decimal places are to be treated as part of the place value system. All too often, teachers will tend to treat operations with decimals in some "new" way and not apply what students already know, the procedures for the operations with whole numbers.

There are some idiosyncrasies with decimals, but by and large the same rules that apply to whole numbers and the four operations apply to decimals.

We have seen in the Activity how using estimation and then placing value concepts assists students in calculating with decimals using paper and pencil. The key here is the absence of any "rules for decimals." Since decimal places which stand for numbers less than one are still part of the overall decimal system that students have learned since first grade, to create a new set of rules creates, in a sense, a new headache for the students.

What has happened here is an excellent example of transfer of learning in which the prior knowledge (use of place value for the four operations with whole numbers) plays a major role in having students understand what is occurring and be able to use similar procedures in computation.

When more complex numbers are involved, such as $0.045 \times 0.67$, the calculator, the tool that the rest of the world uses to compute such products, should be used.

In teaching operations with decimals, be very careful not to try to establish the rule so that more "exotic" types of computations can be completed with paper and pencil. This usually leads to premature "rule intervention" and confusion for those students who need to have less confusion in their mathematics education. There are future years in their education when such ideas can be addressed if they have a sound fundamental understanding.

## Reflections

*Reflecting on the Activity*

1. Was this a lesson in mathematics or in social studies? Explain your response.
2. Why do you think students for this lesson may not have needed manipulatives?

*Reflecting on the Mathematics*

3. Explain why the concepts involved in operations with decimals are the same as those involved with whole numbers.

4. Explain the role of the decimal point in the writing of numbers.
5. What role does estimation play in operations with decimals?

## Reflecting on the Plan

6. Should the traditional rules (lining up decimal places in addition, counting decimal places in the factors when multiplying) be introduced? When?
7. At what point should the calculator be brought into the operations involving decimals?

## Your Reflection

8. What role does rounding, discussed in chapter 3, play in operations with decimals?
9. Do students have to round or can they just estimate? Explain your response.
10. Could Mr. Gardner have made this Activity more student oriented and still attained the objective?
11. How could Mr. Gardner assess the learning of all the students in the room without a test?

# MEASUREMENT

## Make Your Own Ruler

**The Activity**

**Focus: Ms. Hunter has the students develop their own ruler to have them learn what a ruler is and what the numbers on the ruler mean.**

Ms. Hunter gave a number of one-inch strips to each group. "Today, we are going to use these to measure. I am going to give out a lab sheet. Each group is to use inch-strips and measure the objects listed on the sheet."

### Measurement Lab with Inch Strips

A. The width of a floor tile.
B. The width of your mathematics book.
C. The length of your mathematics book.
D. The width of the class door.
E. The width of a window.
F. The height of the teacher's desk.

"I would like each group to begin with a different activity and then do the rest of them in order after that. So, the first group will begin with A and then do B, C, D, E, and F in order. The second group will begin with B and do C next and so on. So, let's get to work. You have 10 minutes."

As the groups began, Ms. Hunter circulated to assist them as well as deal with any confusion and crowding.

When the groups had completed the lab, Ms. Hunter quickly reviewed the answers. She then asked, "Were there any problems?" Michael said, "Measuring the height of the teacher's desk was not easy. We had to hold the strips along the side."

"Good point. Is there any easier way?" Rani said, "Tape them to the desk." The class laughed and then Ms. Hunter said, "That's pretty much what we are going to do." Then the class really laughed. "No, I am not kidding. We are, in a way, going to tape the inch pieces to the things we are measuring."

She picked up strips of green construction paper which were 12 inches long and an inch high. "We are not going to tape the inches to my desk but to these strips. So, everyone, take your glue sticks and as carefully as you can, glue your inch strips on this long strip of paper so that almost none of the green shows through."

As the students did this, Ms. Hunter circulated through the class to offer assistance. As they were nearly completed, she placed a transparency on the overhead. It was similar to what the students were doing, with clear squares on a green strip (to have the clear squares seen, she had a border around each).

She called the class to attention: "So everyone has a strip of 12-inch pieces. Now, I am going to assign each group to redo a certain item on the lab. So, Charisse, your group does item 1. Sid,..." It took a few minutes to assign the items. Then Ms. Hunter said, "Try to count the number of inches beginning with one end of the green strip. It might make it easier." She then had the children move to the task. Throughout the task, Ms. Hunter listened to the counting that students did.

At the end, she said, "Now, I watched as all of you counted the inch-strips on your ruler. Henritta's group began to count by 12s when they measured the door. So now we are going to take that idea and make this a better measuring device."

"We will number each of the inch-strips that are on it. But we will do it so we know which number goes with which strip." With this, Ms. Hunter placed the numeral 1 on the right of the first inch strip. She then said, "I want you to place the numeral 1 where it is here."

| 1 | 2 | 3 | 4 | 5 | | | | | | | |
|---|---|---|---|---|---|---|---|---|---|---|---|

After the students did this, she asked, "Who can come up and place the numbers 2, 3, 4, and 5?" Hands were up immediately. "Oscar?" Oscar came to the overhead and put each of the numbers on the consecutive strips after 1, each number on the right of the strip. "Okay, let's look at what we have," said Ms. Hunter.

| 1 | 2 | 3 | 4 | 5 | 6 | 7 | 8 | 9 | 10 | 11 | 12 |
|---|---|---|---|---|---|---|---|---|----|----|----|

"Great. Katie, would you finish it?" Katie went to the overhead and placed the rest of the numerals in the proper order.

"Math time is just about up. Tonight for homework, you will use your green strip to measure things in your house. Will the secretary in each group come up and get the homework?"

## The Mathematics

Having students know how to use a ruler begins with its construction. Too many times a student is told how to use a ruler properly and yet mistakes are made. Students remember that the number at the right end of a line segment is the length of the line. What they sometimes forget is that this is true only if the left end of the line segment is at

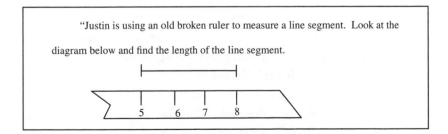

"Justin is using an old broken ruler to measure a line segment. Look at the diagram below and find the length of the line segment.

the left edge of the ruler. Students who do not understand this usually give an incorrect answer to the following.

For an adult with lots of experience with measurement, this is a simple task. The segment begins at 5 and ends at 8. So the distance is 3. However, for some students who think that the answer is always the number at the right end (remember they forget that little fact about beginning at the left end) the answer is 8.

What the students do not understand is that the numbers on a ruler are in a sense ordinals. The numbers on a 12-inch ruler tell you where each individual inch begins and ends as well as what position it has. That is, is it the first, second, or third inch on the ruler? However, without the complete ruler, only the first statement still holds true.

For example, with Justin's broken ruler, the mark at 5 shows the beginning of an inch with the line at 6 showing the end of that inch and the beginning of the next. However, the mark at 5 does not stand for the fifth inch on the ruler. This is what students sometimes forget or maybe have never learned.

By having students construct the ruler and then number it, they engage in developing an understanding of what the numbers mean and how they should be interpreted.

## The Plan

**Title**: Constructing a ruler with 12 inches.

**Teacher Objective**: Students will understand the ruler and what it means and how to use it.

**Objective for Students**: Students will measure with inches.

**NCTM Focal Points 3–5**: Understand how to measure using standard units.

**Materials**: Inch strips; foot strips on green construction paper to create foot ruler; glue or glue sticks; measurement lab; transparency of 12-inch strips on green background.

**Measurement Lab with Inch Strips**:
   Measure:
   A. The width of a floor tile.
   B. The width of your mathematics book.

    C. The length of your mathematics book.

    D. The width of the class door.

    E. The width of a window.

    F. Height of the teacher's desk.

**Homework**: Choose three items in your home and measure them using your ruler. If you can, bring them into school tomorrow to share with the class.

*Beginning Stage*

1. Tell the students that today they will be measuring.
2. Distribute inch strips and measurement lab.
3. Have students complete lab.
   Circulate through the room to monitor the students' work.

*Middle Stage*

4. Discuss the answers from the lab and any difficulties. If none arise, ask how students went about measuring the height of the teacher's desk.
5. Distribute green construction strips and direct students to glue inch pieces on them.
6. Remember to have the students glue the inch pieces as close to end-to-end as they can.
7. Have students use green strips to measure 1 item on list. Assign one group to no. 1, one group to number no. 2, etc.
8. Remind students that it is easier to count the inches if they place one at the end of the ruler and begin from there.
9. When complete, relate how they had to count and recount. If you have overheard anyone stating that there were 12 inches on the green strip, talk about this.
10. Demonstrate for students how to number the first inch on the strip. Use the transparency for this modeling.
11. Have students number inches 2, 3, 4, and 5 on their strips.
12. Using the transparency, have a student show this.
13. Have students complete the numbering of the strip.
14. Have a student demonstrate this using the transparency.

*Final Stage*

> 15. Announce the homework and have the group secretary distribute it.

## Putting It All Together

Measurement cannot be explained. It must be experienced. A teacher can explain the use of a ruler to students but until they actually measure, they still will not fully understand. Also, the ruler is a counting instrument. You count the number of inches (for a customary ruler) that your line comes in contact with. As you can tell from the Activity, simply teaching students to name the number on the ruler is fraught with dangers of misinterpretation. For instruction, having students count the number of inches in many initial activities with the ruler is a way of showing what it can do while reinforcing what linear measure really is, the number of single inches (although they may be glued together) between two points.

## Reflections

*Reflecting on the Activity*

> 1. Why did Ms. Hunter have the students measure with individual inch-strips first?
> 2. What were the students learning about the ruler?

*Reflecting on the Mathematics*

> 3. If Justin were your student, how would you move him to a correct use of the ruler?
> 4. From your experience, give your thoughts on the idea that measurement cannot be taught as we do with other types of learning.
> 5. Comment on this statement: Linear measure is the number of inches that fit between two points.

*Reflecting on the Plan*

6. Why is the Plan specific about things to remind students about?
7. How would you adjust this lesson to teach that there are 3 feet in 1 yard?

*Your Reflection*

8. Many people discuss the idea of a mile, especially for long distances. Do you know how long a mile is? Try this. Think about something you estimate is a mile from your home or school. Drive there. Then check to see how close to a mile you were in your estimate.
9. Discuss the accuracy with your group of student teachers.
10. By the way, time is a similar issue. Using the second hand on a clock, close your eyes and open them when you think 1 minute has gone by. It's the same process, estimation, in two different circumstances. But closer to reality than a workbook page.

# 11

# AREA

## Skipping Through the Rows

**The Activity**

**Focus: Mr. Jensen uses the activity with square tiles to have students understand why multiplication is used to find the area of a rectangle.**

Mr. Jensen began by explaining the work to the students. He said, "Each group is going to get a set of tiles. With them, you will construct a rectangular design using the instructions on the chart paper. Malcolm, would you read these, please?" He displayed chart paper which had the directions for the lesson. Malcolm read, "Using all your squares, construct at least two rectangles where squares with the same color are not touching on sides. Same color tiles can touch at corners. If possible, do not use the same number of tiles for each side of the two rectangles. Draw a diagram of each of your rectangles in your notebooks. Label the rectangles with Roman numerals, I and II."

"Okay," said Mr. Jensen, "you have three minutes. Go." As the students worked in their groups, Mr. Jensen circulated through the groups assessing if the work was being completed according to the directions. Michael raised his hand. "Mr. Jensen, we can only make one type of rectangle." "That's okay," said Mr. Jensen, "you have a special set of tiles. Construct the two rectangles so that the color pattern of the tiles is different in the two rectangles."

As the students finished, Mr. Jensen distributed a data sheet and said, "Record your results on these. Then I want the reporter in each

| Group data sheet | | |
|---|---|---|
| Record the data for each rectangle, I and II. | | |
| Choose one of the rows of squares. | I | II |
| Write the number of squares in that row. | | |
| How many rows of this type? | | |
| How many squares in the rectangle? | | |

| CLASS DATA SHEET | | | |
|---|---|---|---|
| Groups | Number of squares in a row | Number of rows | Number of squares in the rectangle |
| A | | | |
| B | | | |
| C | | | |
| D | | | |
| E | | | |
| F | | | |
| G | | | |
| H | | | |

group to put the results on the data sheet on the overhead projector."
Mr. Jensen then put a copy of the data sheet on the overhead. This
data sheet had enough spaces so that all of the group data could be
seen.

Mr. Jensen moved about the room to help students with the
arrangements especially those who had misread or misinterpreted the

Class Data Sheet

| Groups | | Number of squares in a row | Number of row | Number of squares in the rectangle |
|---|---|---|---|---|
| A | I | 2 | 4 | 8 |
|   | II | 1 | 8 | 8 |
| B | I | 6 | 3 | 18 |
|   | II | 4 | 2 | 18 |
| C | I | 2 | 5 | 10 |
|   | II | 1 | 10 | 18 |
| D | I | 6 | 4 | 24 |
|   | II | 8 | 3 | 24 |
| E | I | 4 | 3 | 12 |
|   | II | 6 | 2 | 12 |
| F | I | 8 | 2 | 16 |
|   | II | 4 | 4 | 16 |
| G | I | 7 | 1 | 7 |
|   | II | 1 | 7 | 7 |
| H | I | 5 | 3 | 15 |
|   | II | 1 | 15 | 15 |

lab directions. As the students began to finish, reporters from the groups began to fill in the chart on the overhead projector. Here is what the chart then looked like.

Mr. Jensen went to the overhead projector and stood next to it. "So, here we have our class data on the lab. Now, in your groups, see if you can find a general pattern for finding the number of squares in a rectangle so that you do not have to make it and count them. You have two minutes. Go."

This did not take the students long. In fact, Mr. Jensen had some problem keeping the students from shouting out the answer. Finally, he called on Gerry. She said, "You multiply."

Mr. Jensen said, "Well that is the operation, but why do you do that?" Frank said, "It's like skip counting. Like in our group, we had three rows of five squares: 5, 10, 15."

Mr. Jensen said, "Frank, what multiplication fact is that?" "3 times 5," he replied.

"Good," said Mr. Jensen. "Now, for homework, I want you to find the number of squares in the rectangles on the homework sheet. I want you to try what Gerry and Frank said here, and then count them to check. Also, tomorrow, we will discuss why Michael's group only had one order of squares in their rectangle."

"Material monitors collect the bags of squares and put them on the supply table. Now, I want everyone to take out their maps from yesterday and find Missouri."

## The Mathematics

In finding area, we find the number of squares (of the same size) which can fit into a closed region. We will now focus on one particular idea, namely how many squares fit into a rectangle and how we can find this amount.

The linkage between the area of a rectangle and multiplication is a natural one which takes into consideration one of the important meanings of multiplication. (Before you go further, you may wish to review this "true idea of multiplication" as we discussed it in chapter 4.) As we saw in chapter 4, when you multiply, the numbers involved mean different things. One number is like a quantitative noun and stands for a certain thing or block of quantity (I have 6 apples in each bag). The other number is like a quantitative adjective and tells you how many of these quantities you have. (I have 4 bags. So, I have 4 × 6 or 24 apples altogether.)

With the area of a rectangle, a similar procedure occurs. The initial step is to see how many squares fit in a row along one side of the rectangle. Once you have established this, then you find how many of these rows you can fit in the rectangle. If your first row contains 5 cm squares and you can construct a total of 7 rows in the figure, then your area is 35 square cm (7 rows of 5 square cm gives you 35 square cm.)

This is the reason why we say that the area of a rectangle is equal to the length times the width. The measurement of the length tells us how many squares are in one row and the measurement of the width tells us how many rows you have (or vice versa). It is never merely the numbers. It is what the numbers mean and what they tell us.

Just some notes on other mathematics. In the Activity, one of groups could only make one rectangle. This was the group of students who had 7 tiles. The reason for this is that they could only make a rectangle with 1 row of 7 squares. When you can only make this 1 row, it indicates that the number is what is called a prime number. In number theory, a prime number is a number which has only two factors, itself and 1. So, if there was a group with 11 squares, the same thing would occur.

Also, one of the groups which had 16 squares not only made a rectangle (2 by 8) but also made a square with 4 squares on each side. As a teacher, you could use this geometric/measurement idea to introduce the linkage between the idea of square in measurement to the idea of a "square number," a number which has a pair of factors where the factors are equal. For example, in this activity, the students with 16 squares had a square with 4 squares on each side. The area is 16 squares or $4 \times 4$ which many times is written as $4^2$.

This idea of integrating topics helps the students remember the relationship.

## The Plan

**Title**: Introducing the area of a rectangle.

**Teacher Objective**: Students will learn the formula for the area of a rectangle.

**Objective for Students**: How many squares will fit in a rectangle? How can you find this without the rectangle in front of you?

**NCTM Focal Points 3–5**: Select and apply appropriate standard units and tool to measure area.

**Materials**: Square tiles in sets of: 7, 8, 10, 12, 15, 16, 18, 24. Group data, class data sheet on overhead transparency; chart paper: "Using all your squares, construct at least two rectangles where squares with the same color are not touching on sides. Same color tiles can touch at corners. If possible, do not use the same number of tiles for each side of the two rectangles. Draw a diagram of each of your rectangles in your notebooks. Label the rectangles with Roman numerals, I and II."

**Homework**: For each rectangle, draw a diagram and find the number of tiles. Then use multiplication or skip counting to verify the answer.

   1. Length = 10, Width = 4; 2. Length = 9, Width = 7; 3. Length = 12, Width = 3.

*Beginning Stage*

   1. Distribute sets of tiles to student groups. Ask the students to make as many rectangles as they can, drawing diagrams of each. As students begin to work, circulate and distribute the group data sheet. Be aware of the students with 7 tiles who will only have 1 rectangle.

*Middle Stage*

   2. Have recorder from each group complete data on class data sheet at overhead.
   3. Ask students to study the data sheet and look for patterns with the relationship of the length/width of rectangle and number of tiles to fill it.
   4. Discuss patterns in terms of skip counting/multiplication.

*Final Stage*

   5. Give directions for the homework. Have students collect materials.

**Doing Some Mathematics**

   1. Maria takes 12 1-inch squares and makes the following design. What is the area of the design?

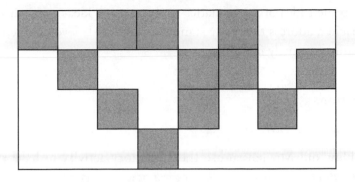

2. Find the area of a rectangle that is 4 inches wide and 7 inches long. Draw a diagram and draw squares to validate your answer.
3. Take the diagram in no. 2 and draw a diagonal from one corner to the other. What is the area of each of the triangles formed? Explain your answer.
4. In the design in no. 1, find the area of the white enclosed part.

## Putting It All Together

For many people, area is always "length times width" no matter the shape of the figure. Area is a very important concept and formula in mathematics, so it must be introduced to students in an understandable way. This lesson takes the students' knowledge of multiplication (skip counting) and uses it to develop the area of a rectangle. Again, as an initial learning lesson, it is important that the students investigate and analyze the ideas involved before they are formalized or, as in this case, semiformalized. From this point, the next lesson could move to introducing the ideas of length and width as well as reinforcing why multiplication is the functional operation. You see again here an inductive view of mathematics.

Also, in the Mathematics section, the discussion about prime numbers and square numbers shows that there are topics in mathematics which can, and should, be integrated. This helps the students develop their idea of mathematics as interwoven ideas and helps you, the teacher, address the many standards in a grade level mathematics program in a timely fashion.

## Reflections

*Reflecting on the Activity*

1. How did Mr. Jensen use the laboratory activity to have the students establish the idea of area of a rectangle?
2. How did the lesson use nontechnical language (language of understanding) to have students focus on the concept?
3. What would be the theme of the next lesson on area?

*Reflecting on the Mathematics*

4. Explain in your own words why area of a rectangle is found using multiplication.
5. In finding the area of a rectangle, what is the difference between $4 \times 7$ and $7 \times 4$?
   Does this "lack" of difference occur in all applications of multiplication?

*Reflecting on the Plan*

(Reflections 7 and 8 ask you to consider how to develop the idea of prime and square numbers into the study of area.)

6. How did Mr. Jensen move the students to understand that area means all the squares that fit?
7. How could Mr. Jensen use the lessons on area of a rectangle to be a review of multiplication facts?
8. When could Mr. Jensen relate the word *square* as used in measurement to *square* as used in arithmetic or algebra, such as $7^2$?
9. When could Mr. Jensen use this lesson to introduce the idea of prime numbers to the students?

*Your Reflections*

10. Why is it important for students to construct the area of rectangles before they move to the formal language of the formula?

11. Explain how you could say that "Area means all the squares that would fit into a shape."

12. How would you use the explanation in no. 11 to discuss area of other figures?

# 12
## VOLUME

## It's Like Looking at an Apartment House…

### The Activity

**Focus: Ms. Collins introduces students to the concept of volume of a rectangular prism and why multiplication is used in the formula for finding its volume.**

As the class began, Ms. Collins had a set of 20 1-inch cubes on the front table. When she flipped the objective sheet, she had Maxine read it: "How many apartments are in the apartment house?" she said. Ms. Collins then told the class that today they were going to look at simple structures and investigate the mathematics in the construction.

She called Emil to the table and said, "Emil, as I discuss my apartment house, I want you to build it. Class, you are to evaluate Emil's construction. Here we go. I have two apartments across the front of the building. Let's have them face the class. Behind each of these, there are two other apartments. Finally, the building has two floors."

Emil built the structure using the cubes. "So what is the information about this building? It has two apartments across the front. Now, how many down the side?" "Two," yelled Ned. "Come up and count them," said Ms. Collins. As Ned counted, he realized that the apartment in the front line also counted along the side. "Nope, there are three down the side," he said. "Good, Ned, now tell us how many floors." "Two."

"Girls and boys, remember as you do this work to fully count all the apartments across the front, down the side and then the number of floors."

"Now, Emil, begin to count the apartments," said Ms. Collins. Emil began to count the blocks by removing them from the structure. He finally stopped and said, "There are 12 blocks so there are 12 apartments."

"So, if we have two apartments along the front, three apartments along the side and two floors, we have 12 apartments. Thanks, Emil. You can rejoin your group." In doing so, Emil got high-fives from his partners.

"Now, each group will be given an apartment house to build and then we will collect the data on a chart. After everyone is done, we will discuss the data."

Ms. Collins then asked the materials monitors to distribute the blocks to each group. While this was being done, she asked for each recorder to obtain a lab sheet from the OUTBOX at the front table. There was a different description on each of the six lab sheets for the groups.

"Okay, get to work. You have four minutes." In this time, Ms. Collins first circulated through the room to help with any questions. Then, she put an acetate sheet on the overhead projector which had the chart:

| Group | Number of apartments across the front | Number of apartments down the side | Number of floors in the building | Total number of apartments |
|-------|---------------------------------------|------------------------------------|----------------------------------|----------------------------|
| A     |                                       |                                    |                                  |                            |
| B     |                                       |                                    |                                  |                            |
| C     |                                       |                                    |                                  |                            |
| D     |                                       |                                    |                                  |                            |
| E     |                                       |                                    |                                  |                            |
| F     |                                       |                                    |                                  |                            |

As groups completed the work, Ms. Collins asked the reporter in each group to fill in the chart for the group. When the chart was completed, Ms. Collins called the class to attention.

| Group | Number of apartments across the front | Number of apartments down the side | Number of floors in the building | Total number of apartments |
|---|---|---|---|---|
| A | 2 | 4 | 4 | 32 |
| B | 3 | 2 | 4 | 24 |
| C | 4 | 3 | 3 | 36 |
| D | 5 | 2 | 2 | 20 |
| E | 3 | 2 | 3 | 18 |
| F | 4 | 5 | 2 | 40 |

"Here are the results. Now, in your groups, I want you to develop a connection between the columns of numbers. In doing this, I want you to explain why this occurs. So, you just cannot say, 'Add' but tell me why you would add, if adding will help."

"You have three minutes. Go!!!"

When time was up, Ms. Collins said, "Whose group would like to report? Robin?" "We were group F. In our building, we had four apartments across the front, five down the side, and the building had two floors. So, we built the first floor and found that we had 20 apartments. So we said we can find this by multiplication. Then, since we had two floors in the building, we said that we had 20 apartments two times. So, two times 20 is 40. So there are 40 apartments in the building."

Ms. Collins asked two other groups to report and the class heard similar ideas. Finally, Ms. Collins asked, "Who can write a formula for this? Diego?" Diego moved to the board and wrote, "F × S × FL = Apartments."

"Diego, what do the variables stand for?" "F is the number of apartments along the front, S is the number of apartments down the side, and FL is the number of floors in the building."

"Diego, would you please write it in large symbols on the chart paper. We will tape it up on the wall so we can use it for our work." As Diego wrote the formula, Ms. Collins read along so that the class again heard the formula and the meaning of each symbol.

"Now, tomorrow, after you practice this idea for homework, we will discuss where this fits into our study of geometry and measurement. But right now, paper monitors in each group: Please pick up tonight's homework. While they are doing that, please take out the play we were reading yesterday. On the chart paper, I have written who will be playing each part today."

### The Mathematics

Simply put, to find the volume of an object, you take cubes of the same size and find how many cubes you need to build the object. In the lesson, Ms. Collins used inch cubes since they are easier to handle.

For example, the structure below has a volume of 7 cubic inches (assuming we are using cubes which are 1 inch on each side.)

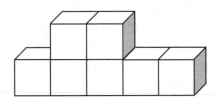

Why does it have a volume of 7 cubic inches?  Because it is made up of 7 cubes. Here is a structure which is also 7 cubic inches. (By the way, can you find the cube that seems to be "hidden"?)

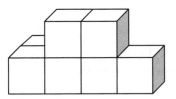

When you have a rectangular solid, the procedure becomes more efficient since you do not have to count. Here is a model that we will use for an example (and that Ms. Collins used for homework). We want to find the number of cubes in the rectangular solid. Let's think of the model as an apartment house where each cube is an apartment. Take some cubes and construct the rectangular solid. You could use bouillon cubes if you wish.

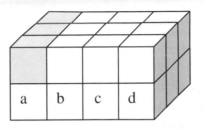

On the first floor, we have 4 apartments across the front. For each of the apartments in front, a, b, c, d, there are two apartments behind each of them. So, on the first floor, we have 3 rows of 4 apartments each. We have 3 sets of 4 (or 3 fours as in chapter 4 on skip counting) which gives us 12 apartments on the first floor. In this way, we have multiplied the length across the front of the apartment house by the width going down the side (L × W).

But, our apartment house has 2 floors. Its height is 2. So we have two sets of 12 or 24 apartments.

To sum it up (no pun intended) we multiplied the length (L) by the width (W) (to find the number of apartments on the first floor), and then multiplied that answer (product) by the height (H) to find the number of apartments in the entire building.

In mathematical terms, we say, we multiplied the length by the width by the height to find the number of cubes in the structure. This total number of cubes is called the volume of the structure.

In many texts, you will see the formula V = B × h, where B stands for the area of the Base of the structure. The value of B is actually the volume of the first floor. This means that the numerical value of

B (area of the Base of the structure) and the volume of the first floor are the same. However, mathematically, the idea of using the area of the Base as a part of the volume formula does not relate to students what the number really means; that is, the number of cubes on the first floor.

You could think of the formula as: $V = V_1 \times h$, where $V_1$ is the volume of the first floor. Then the students have an understanding of why the length and width are multiplied, to find the number of cubes on the first level.

## The Plan

**Title**: Introducing the formula for volume of a rectangular solid.

**Teacher Objective**: Students will learn how to find the volume of a rectangular solid.

**Objective for Students**: By building structures with cubes, you will find the number of cubes in the entire structure.

**NCTM Focal Points 3–5**: Select and apply appropriate standard units and tool to measure volume.

**Materials**: 20 cubes for demonstration at beginning of class. Sets of 20 cubes for each group.

Structures to be built by students: Placed on cards in OUTBOX.

|     | Front | Side | Floors |
|-----|-------|------|--------|
| a.  | 2     | 4    | 4      |
| b.  | 3     | 2    | 4      |
| c.  | 4     | 3    | 3      |
| d.  | 5     | 2    | 2      |
| e.  | 3     | 2    | 3      |
| f.  | 4     | 5    | 2      |

**Homework**: If I build an apartment house that has 4 apartments across the front, 3 down the side, and it has 2 floors, how many apartments are there?

*Beginning Stage*

1. Choose a student. Have the student build an apartment house type structure (rectangular solid). Use 2 across by 4 down with 2 floors. Have the student count the number of cubes (apartments) in the structure.

*Middle Stage*

2. Have recorder in each group select a lab sheet with the dimensions written on it from the OUTBOX.
3. Have groups construct their apartments.
4. Have recorder fill in the Group Data Sheet.
5. Have the students work in groups and look for a pattern from the sheet. (If there is no response, move them through one of the examples as a class.)

*Final Stage*

6. When the relationship is established, have the students approximate a formula using whatever symbolic representation that is adequate and correct.
7. Have recorders pick up homework for members of the group.

---

Homework: How many apartments are in this apartment house? Explain two ways of finding your answer.

### Doing Some Mathematics

1. Rodney creates a structure that has 8-inch cubes as the base, 5-inch cubes on a second level and 4 cubes on a third level. What is the volume of this structure?
2. Create 3 structures which have a volume of 36 cubic inches.
3. Explain why the maximum volume of the rectangular solid made with 54-inch cubes is 54 cubic inches.
4. Explain why the formula for the volume of a rectangular solid is:

    Length × Width × Height where these are the dimensions of the solid.


### Putting It All Together

Volume is the way we measure the amount of space in a 3-dimensional space, such as a room. In teaching students about volume, there is a need to keep their attention on the concept and not allow them to confuse it with area. As a result, area and volume should not be taught together.

The use of models in the teaching of volume is very important since 3-dimentional ideas need hands-on representation. In doing this, the students begin to understand the impact of each of the 3 dimensions and the role they play in determining the volume.

The use of the apartment house model gives the students a way of reconstructing the idea of volume without making it just another formula.


### Reflections

*Reflecting on the Activity*

1. Why does Ms. Collins use introductory language and symbols to introduce the concept?
2. Why did she not have Diego use L, W, and H for his variables when he wrote the formula?

*Reflecting on the Mathematics*

3. In your own words, explain what you mean by volume.
4. How is volume related to area and how are these different?

*Reflecting on the Plan*

5. Why is the use of an apartment house a good way of addressing volume?
6. In a subsequent lesson, how would you make the transition from the introductory to formal language such as the word *Volume* and the formula?
7. If students just have a knowledge of formulas, what do you think they would get as an incorrect answer for no. 1 in the Doing Some Mathematics section of this chapter?

*Your Reflections*

8. In this Activity, explain why the teacher must be very organized.
9. What are the essential ideas that you want the students to have after this lesson?

# 13

## MEAN

### How Much Does Each Get?

**The Activity**

**Focus: Ms. Clausen uses an activity by which students can understand the concept of the mean of a set of data while setting the stage for the development of the formula.**

As the students got ready for mathematics class, Ms. Clausen distributed the index cards which were used during the median lesson. She then asked for the students to form up in their groups of four. While the students did this, Ms. Clausen asked the supply member of each group to get a set of base-ten blocks. Ms Clausen then said, "We are going to let the number on the card stand for the amount of money you spent in a candy store. You will need your base-ten blocks in order to complete the work on your group lab sheet." She then handed out the lab sheet and began to circulate around the room. "You have 10 minutes to complete the lab."

When all the procedures were on the board, Ms. Clausen asked each group to analyze all the procedures and discuss how they are similar and different, giving them five minutes to do this. At the end of the time, she asked reporters to give their group's analysis. Melissa said that two of the groups kept moving the base-ten blocks until they all had an equal amount. "Good," said Ms. Clausen. Monique's and Todd's groups did this. "Any other method?" Derek said, "There are groups that put all their materials in the center, shared out the tens,

---

### Sharing Quantities:

1. Each student will use the base ten blocks to represent the number on their card.
2. Then without speaking, share out the blocks so that at the end of the sharing, each member of the group has the same amount of blocks in front of them.
3. When this is done, decide on what exactly the group did and have the recorder write out your group's procedure.
4. Have the Reporter member of the group write the group's procedure on the board.

NOTE: If you do not have enough tens to share out equally, trade them in for ones.

---

and then shared out the ones. Also, in Phil's group, before they shared out the ones, they had to trade 2 tens for 20 ones."

"So," Ms. Clausen said, "We have two methods. What I want you to do in your groups is to write a rule for each of these two methods. Let's take about five minutes to do this." As the groups worked, Ms. Clausen moved through the room to assist as needed. Jonathan raised his hand and said, "It's hard to write a rule for the moving around idea. It just is a matter of moving things around until they are equal. Is that all it is?" "We'll find out in a few minutes," responded Ms. Clausen.

After the time was up, the class discussed the rules they had made. Again, Jonathan's problem was raised by other groups. "All you say is, 'Move things around until everyone has the same amount'." "Okay," said Ms. Clausen, "How about another method?"

Terrence said, "Put all the pieces together and then share them out evenly." "Great," said Ms. Clausen. "Now let's use math words. When you put things together, what is that called?" "Addition" the class answered. "So," Ms Clausen said, "The first procedure is to add," and she wrote the word *Add* on the board.

"Now, when we share numbers of things out equally, what do we call that?" "Division," said the class. "Good," she said as she wrote *Division* under the word *Add* on the board.

She then placed the following prewritten problem on the overhead. "Three friends collect juice cans to recycle. Marisa collected 25. Joe collected 32, and Regina collected 33. If they share them equally, how many juice cans will each have?" "So, here is a problem on the overhead. Use your materials and this procedure to solve this. Then work with each other to use paper and pencil to solve it. Then compare your answers." Ms. Clausen circulated through the class until time for science arrived. "When you finish, put the written answer in your notebooks for tomorrow's class. Also, I have a set of two homework problems for you to solve. Take one while we get set for science." She then asked the supply members of each group to return the tens and ones to the cabinet and bring a set of beakers back to the groups for the science lesson.

## The Mathematics

One of the most difficult questions I ask my classes or teachers during workshops is, "What does the 'mean' tell us?" All of them can tell me how to find the mean. But few if any have ever been able to fully explain what it tells us about the data.

The mean simply tells us how much each of us would receive if we all pooled our quantities and shared the total out equally. For example, we might collect aluminum cans and decide that the money we make from the refund will be shared equally. We might have a different number of cans. You could have 25, I could have 15, and Miriam (our mutual friend) could have 35. This gives us a total of 75 cans. So each of us would get 25 cans to bring to the refund center.

More formally, the mean of a data set tells us what each data point would have if the total of the data involved were shared equally. Match this sentence against the preceding paragraph to truly understand why you need to understand mathematics before you can formalize it.

And now the question, "So??" What does it tell us if we know how much each person gets when the total quantity is shared out equally?

In the analysis of statistics, the mean does not stand alone as a single entity. Alone it tells us very little. However, use it as one indicator with other indicators such as the median and you begin to see patterns in the data. Such analysis is not the scope of this book. However, it is something you should seek to learn as you begin to teach concepts such as the mean in your classroom.

Remember. There are no jobs for "Mean Finders" in the world. However, there are numerous careers for people who are able to use the mean and other types of statistics to analyze data. That is a goal for your students and therefore of your teaching.

### The Plan

**Title**: Introduce the concept of the mean of a set of data.

**Teacher Objective**: Students will understand the concept of mean and its relationship to the formula for finding the mean for a set of data.

**Objective for Students**: How many different methods can we use to share quantities so everyone gets an equal amount?

**NCTM Focal Points 3–5**: Describe the important features of a set of data.

**Materials**: Index cards from median activity; base-ten materials; lab sheet.

**Overhead Transparency**: Three friends collect juice cans to recycle. Marisa collected 25. Joe collected 32, and Regina collected 33. If they share them equally, how many juice cans will each have?

---

### Sharing Quantities:

1. Each student will use the base ten blocks to represent the number on their card.
2. Then without speaking, share out the blocks so that at the end of the sharing, each member of the group has the same amount of blocks in front of them.
3. When this is done, decide on what exactly the group did and have the recorder write out your group's procedure.
4. Have the Reporter member of the group write the group's procedure on the board.

NOTE: If you do not have enough tens to share out equally, trade them in for ones.

**Homework**: Answer each question using a complete sentence.

1. Zum-Bars were one of the snacks at a party. At the end of the party, there were 15 Zum-Bars in one bowl, 19 in a second bowl, and 26 in a third bowl. It was decided that Ms. Clausen's class and Mr. Gyles class would share the leftover candy equally. How many pieces of candy did each class receive?

2. In collecting change around the house, Marnie found 45 cents, Arthur found 65 cents, and Sam found 37 cents. If they share the change equally, how much will each person receive?

*Beginning Stage*

1. Distribute index cards from median lesson.
2. Ask supply members to get sets of tens and ones from the cabinet.
3. Tell students that the number on the card will show the number of cents they spent at the store. Distribute the lab sheet.
4. Give the students 10 minutes to complete the lab.
5. Circulate through the room during the lab.

*Middle Stage*

6. As students complete the lab, have each recorder write the procedure used on the board.
7. Discuss the methods with the class. Make sure that the methods are mathematically correct.
8. Look for a method which puts everything together and shares the total out equally.
9. If this method does not occur, have the groups use it to see if the answer is the same as theirs.
10. Bring out the idea that the "putting together" is adding and the "sharing" is division.
11. Place transparency on overhead and have the groups solve it first with materials and then with paper and pencil.

*Final Stage*

12. Circulate through the class to assist. Ask them to put the finished work in their notebooks.
13. Remember to use this at the beginning of tomorrow's class as a warm-up/review.

## Doing Some Mathematics

1. In your own words, describe what the mean of a set of data shows. Do not use the formula for finding the mean in your explanation.
2. Without using materials, what is the mean of 5, 7, and 9? How did you determine this?
3. Use base-ten blocks to find the mean of 27, 38, 46, 52, and 19.
4. How does your procedure in no. 3 give us the formula for finding the mean?
5. Explain the difference between the median (chapter 2) and the mean for a set of data.

## Putting It All Together

The mean is one of the important basic ideas in statistics in the school curriculum. Another, the median, was addressed in chapter 2. Why not together? As we have said before, when two ideas are so close together in meaning, it is better to teach them separately so students do not confuse them.

The mean in a set of data tells us how much each person should get if the total of the data is shared out equally (or evenly).

The format of the lesson gives the students experience with the accumulation/sharing idea so that the mean begins to make sense in terms of what it tells us. In many instances, the mean is taught without such work so all students come away with is that to find the mean, you add and divide.

With this lesson and the work with the median, students are getting ready to use both of these ideas to do what statistics education in the schools is all about: analysis of data in decision making. Just being able to find the middle number or the mean does not help students realize the reason for learning statistical concepts.

## Reflections

*Reflecting on the Activity*

1. How does Ms. Clausen inductively develop the formula for the mean?
2. How does she keep the students from focusing on the arithmetic of the mean?

*Reflecting on the Mathematics*

3. How does the mean differ from the median?
4. Why are both called Measures of Central Tendency?
5. Create a data set where the mean and median are equal.
6. Create a data set where the mean and median are not equal.

*Reflecting on the Plan*

7. In the plan, why did Ms. Clausen include the examples she would give?
8. How was she going to use today's lesson as a beginning for the next lesson?

*Your Reflections*

9. What does the lesson help the students understand about the mean?
10. What confusion could arise if the mean and median are taught at the same time?
11. Explain why in finding the mean you add all the data together and then divide.
12. How is this lesson inductive and not deductive?

# 14

# PERCENT

## Leveling the Field of Comparison

### The Activity

**Focus: Ms. Levy uses a scale for proportion to introduce students to the concept of percent and its use in problem solving.**

Ms. Levy distributed the grid as she spoke to the class (see Figure 14.1). "Today we will spend the first part of the class constructing a problem solving grid and then we will solve some problems using it." She then placed an acetate copy on the overhead and continued. "You have two columns. The one on the right is calibrated by 5 from 0 to 100. The left column has a 0 opposite the 0 in the right column. At the top of the left column opposite the 100, I want you to write 800. What we are now going to do is fill in the left column using simple arithmetic and its relation to the right column."

"For example, Audrey, on the left side, what number is halfway between 0 and 800?" "400," Audrey replied. "Good, now on the chart, where would I place the 400?"

Jeffrey raised his hand and said, "You count the spaces, take half of them and count up from 0. That's where 400 would go." "Okay, anyone else? Max?"

"Since 50 is halfway between 0 and 100 on the right side, I would place 400 opposite the 50." "Okay, anyone else?" When no one responded, Ms. Levy said, "Both procedures will get the job done. However, which is more efficient and quicker?" "Max's" the students said.

"So, write 400 opposite the 50. I will do this on the overhead so you have a model" (see Figure 14.2). After a minute or so, Ms. Levy

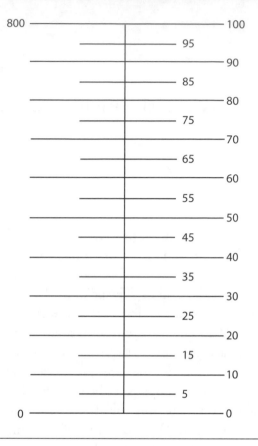

**Figure 14.1**

said, "I want you to work in your groups to answer the questions I have written on the chart paper. When you feel you are correct, write them on your grid. Here they are."

On the chart paper, there were four questions:

1. What is number halfway between 0 and 400?
2. Where would it be placed on the grid?
3. What number is halfway between 400 and 800?
4. Where would it be placed on the grid?

Ms. Levy circulated through the room to keep the students on task and to answer any questions. When she observed that the groups were finished, she said, "Miguel, go to the overhead and explain your answers to questions 1 and 2."

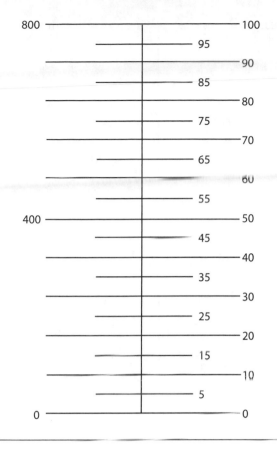

Figure 14.2

Miguel moved to the overhead and said, "Two hundred is halfway between 0 and 400. Now, 400 is opposite 50 and 0 is opposite 0. So, we placed 200 opposite 25 because 25 is halfway between 50 and 0." With that, Miguel wrote 200 opposite 25 on the overhead grid.

"Very good," said Ms. Levy. "Now what about questions 3 and 4?" Ms. Levy then called on Rosalie who went to the overhead and placed "600" opposite "75" using a explanation similar to that of Miguel (see Figure 14.3)

"Now, let's move your groups to another set of questions and then the grid will be set up for problem solving. Here they are. Again, when you are sure you are correct, write them on your grid." She then uncovered another piece of chart paper which had two questions.

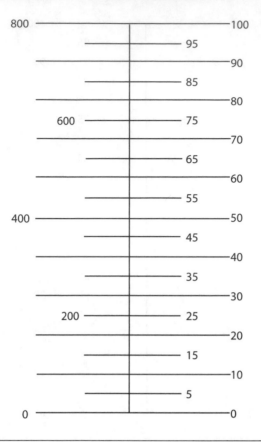

**Figure 14.3**

5. What numbers would you place on the grid between 0 and 200?

6. Where would you place each of them? Why?

"Okay, go," she said. And the students began to work.

In a few minutes, Ms. Levy said, "Gerry, would you go to the overhead and place your numbers on the left side of the grid?" When Gerry was done, Ms. Levy asked how she arrived at the answer. Gerry said, "Since there were 5 spaces between 0 and 200, each space was worth 40. So I used the numbers 40, 80, 120, and 160" (see Figure 14.4).

"So," said Ms. Levy, "now that we know that each space is equal to 40, I want you to fill in the rest of the grid. Use your calculators if you wish. You have four minutes. Go."

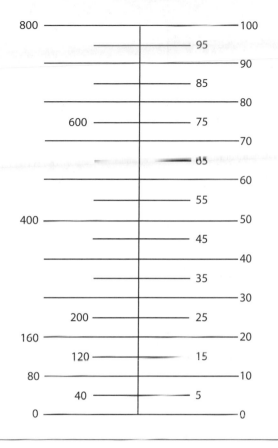

**Figure 14.4**

After the students completed the work, Ms. Levy placed a completed grid on the overhead projector and said, "Check your work against this and correct any errors on your grid. Then, we'll talk about it" (see Figure 14.5).

"Now, let's talk about how we use the grid. Eric, what do we have on the left side of the grid?" asked Ms. Levy. "The numbers from 0 to 800." "And Tom on the right side?" "The numbers from 0 to 100."

Ms. Levy uncovered a piece of chart paper. It read, "7. Look at 160 on the left. Why is it related to 20 on the right?" "I want you to discuss this with your groups. You have one minute. Go."

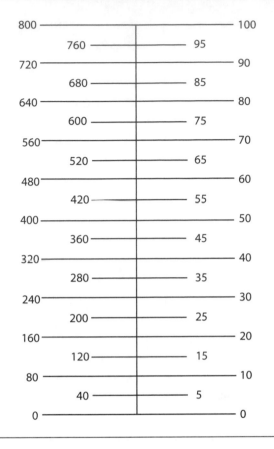

**Figure 14.5**

Soon, Ms. Levy was receiving very interesting looks from the students. "Martha, what is the problem?" "Nothing" said Martha, "It's just that the question is so easy." "Yes it is" said Ms. Levy.

"Go ahead, Martha." "Well, 160 is related to 20 because they are the same distance up the scale from zero."

"Good," said Ms. Levy. "But now here is an important vocabulary part. Here is the way we say this in mathematics." With that, she placed an overlay on the overhead which read, "20% of 800 is 160."

"Now, let's stop talking about it and look at some applications. I am going to give each pairs of students three problems: Work together to find the answer."

With this, Ms. Levy distributed problem sets to each group and began to move about the room to assist them.

1. Harry collected $800 and was allowed to keep 20%. How much money did John keep?
2. There are 800 people in a survey. 40% say that they like Zum candy bars. How many people said they like Zum candy bars?
3. From the information in no. 2, how many people said they did not like Zum candy bars? What percent of the people in the survey said that they did not like Zum candy bars?

She allowed the students to use the rest of the time to discuss and work on the three problems. As the session time ended, she said, "Bring those examples to class tomorrow and we will use them to help us move on to the next step of percent."

## The Mathematics

Percent is used as a way of relating a portion of a quantity. When someone says, "My taxes are 20% of my salary," they mean that out of every $100 in salary, they pay $20 in taxes. That means that the person really gets $80 in their paycheck. Percent is also used to compare portions of two different quantities. For example, 30% of 600 is less than 70% of 300 because 30% of 600 is 180 and 70% of 300 is 210.

Whichever way percent is used, it is the comparing of a quantity to 100. The use of the grid in the lesson shows this. If the total on the left was 1200 or 30, the right side of the grid would still be 0 to 100 and the left side would be calibrated accordingly.

To find a percent of a number, you set up the grid and, with the left side based on the total, find the percent opposite the part of the total. For example, find 35% of 40. Let's look at the grid (see Figure 14.6).

In looking at the grid, 35 on the percent (right) side of the grid matches with 14. So, 35% of 40 is 14.

To find the number which is a percent of a total, you calibrate the grid and then look for the number matching to the percent. For

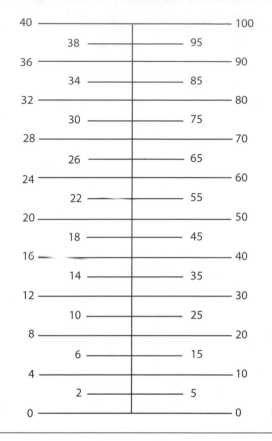

**Figure 14.6**

example, 176 is what percent of 320? Let's look at the grid (see Figure 14.7). From the grid you can see that 176 is 55% of 320. There are further refinements of the grid which would then help you solve percent applications even when there are fractional percent.

Also, it is confusing to say, "Percent means out of 100" since this gives you the idea that you are dealing with a quantity of 100% or less. For example, it is not easy to deal with the idea of 130% of 800 if the idea of percent meaning out of 100 is your basis. Actually, 130% means I have 100% and another 30%. So, using the example from the Activity, 130% of 800 means I have 100% of 800 (which is 800)

| 320 | | 100 |
|---|---|---|
| | 304 | 95 |
| 288 | | 90 |
| | 272 | 85 |
| 256 | | 80 |
| | 240 | 75 |
| 224 | | 70 |
| | 208 | 65 |
| 192 | | 60 |
| | 176 | 55 |
| 160 | | 50 |
| | 144 | 45 |
| 128 | | 40 |
| | 112 | 35 |
| 96 | | 30 |
| | 80 | 25 |
| 64 | | 20 |
| | 48 | 15 |
| 32 | | 10 |
| | 16 | 5 |
| 0 | | 0 |

**Figure 14.7**

and 30% of 800 (which is 240) for a total of 1040. So, 130% of 800 is 1040.

Another way of looking at percent is as a ratio. In the first example above (see Figure 14.6), you want to find 35% of 40. This means you want to find the number on the left scale (the 40 scale) that is at the same level as 35 on the 100 (or %) scale. Here, you can have the grid help create a proportion.

In this case the □ represents the answer; that is, the number which is 35% of 40. So, the proportion is based on the position that each part of the problem has on the grid (see Figure 14.8).

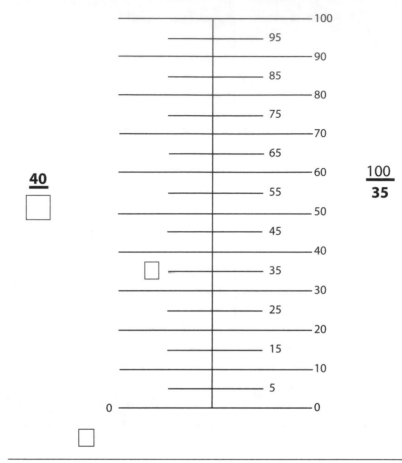

**Figure 14.8**

You have

$$\frac{40}{\square} = \frac{100}{35}$$

So,   $40 * 35 = 100 * \square$

$1400 = 100 * \square$

So,   $14 = \square$

That means that 14 is 35% of 40.

In this way, the grid leads to the proportional methods for solving percent problems.

## The Plan

**Title**: Introduction of percent.

**Teacher Objective**: Introduce the concept and use of percent through a proportional scaling process.

**Objective for Students**: Using 100 as a tool for comparison.

**NCTM Focal Points**: Work flexibly with percents to solve problems. Develop, analyze, and explain methods of solving problems involving proportions such as scaling.

**Materials**: Grid model (see Appendix A) A with 100 and 800 at top.

Transparency of Grid model A with 100 and 800 at top.

Grid model B completely filled in on left side.

Transparency of Grid model B completely filled in on left side.

Transparency with "20% of 800 is 160" written on it.

Four questions on chart paper:
1. What is number halfway between 0 and 400?
2. Where would it be placed on the grid?
3. What number is halfway between 400 and 800?
4. Where would it be placed on the grid?

Next two questions on chart paper:
5. What numbers would you place on the grid between 0 and 200?
6. Where would you place each of them? Why?

Next question on chart paper
7. Look at 160 on the left. Why is it related to 20 on the right?

*Beginning Stage*

1. Distribute Grid model A to each student and place transparency on the overhead.
   a. Explain the sides of the grid.

2. Use placement of 400 on the left side to have students understand how numbers are placed on the left side.
   a. Use Transparency of Grid model A to have students record
   the results and check their work.

*Middle Stage*

3. Use Questions 1 to 4 to assess students' knowledge of using
grid to place quantities with placement of 200 and 600 as the
primary examples.
   a. Use Questions 5 and 6 to have students work in groups to
   compute and place numbers between 0 and 200 on the left
   side of the grid.
   b. Have students assess their work by having a student complete this part of the grid.
   c. Have students use this information to complete scaling of
   left side of grid.
   d. Use Transparency of grid B to have students check their
   work.

*Final Stage*

4. Use 160 on the left side and 20 on the right side to introduce
the percent statement:
   a. 20% of 800 is 160.
   b. Have students work on the three problems and remind
   them to bring them to class tomorrow.

## Doing Some Mathematics

Use the percent grid to solve these exercises.

1. Find 65% of 1200
2. Find 45% of 60
3. Find 85% of 1,000
4. What % of 200 is 120?
5. What % of 860 is 258?
6. What % of 5,000 is 2,000?
7. Which is better: 35% of 800 or 70% of 400? Explain your
answer.

## Putting It All Together

The use of percent is one of the basic needs if one is to have good quantitative literacy skills. To accomplish this, students need to have facility with juggling numbers as opposed to just strict computing. This type of lesson, as well as many of those you have worked with in this book, give the students a personal use of the ideas, a necessary ingredient in any true learning and quantitative literacy.

Most people learn percent in terms of "cases." You can find these in most mathematics books. This calls for strict "remembering." However, in this lesson, students work with the idea of percent and then acquire the ability to reconstruct the application if forgotten. The same cannot be true about memorization.

Teaching students percent in an understandable fashion and having them acquire flexibility with the concept and associated skills gives them a knowledge which will give them a mathematical appreciation of percent and its uses that mere remembering replication of models cannot do.

## Reflections

*Reflecting on the Activity*

1. How much time did Mr. Levy speak to the class before they were actively involved in the lesson?
2. What had Mr. Levy established by the time he allowed the students to work in groups?

*Reflecting on the Mathematics*

3. In your own words, explain what is meant by percent.
4. Why is the idea that percent means "out of 100" not a good way of approaching it with students?
5. What does 150% of 40 mean?

*Reflecting on the Plan*

6. How did Ms. Levy's preparation of the transparencies and chart paper keep the lesson moving?

7. Why did she not tell the students the entire "percent" story in this lesson?

*Your Reflections*

8. In a mathematics book or mathematics methods book, look up the idea of number sense. Explain how number sense plays a role in this lesson.

9. How does this approach differ from the way that you learned how the use percent?

10. How would you explain that this is a student centered activity?

# 15

## ORDER OF OPERATIONS

### An Agreement? Did you get the Memo?

**The Activity**

**Focus: Ms. Lewis uses the knowledge that students have of real life applications of mathematics to have them understand initial ideas with the Order of Operations.**

Ms. Lewis began the lesson by having students discuss the homework problem. "Jonathan, come up to the overhead and show what you did for homework."

"Well, I used the sales' page of the newspaper and bought 5 pens for $3 each and 4 notebooks for $2 each. I then multiplied 5 × $3 for a total of $15 and 4 × $2 for a total of $8. Then I added $15 and $8 and got a total of $23."

"Excellent," said Ms. Lewis. "Aretha, what did you do?" Aretha walked to the overhead projector and explained, "I bought two dictionaries, Spanish and Chinese, for $8 each and 3 books about different planets for $5 each. Like Jonathan, I first multiplied to find the cost of the dictionaries, so 2 times $8 is $16 and then I multiplied to find the cost of the books on planets. So, 3 times $5 for a total of $15. Then I added $16 and $15 for a total of $31."

"Nicely done," said Ms. Lewis. "Now what I want you to do is work in your groups and decide on a way of solving all problems of this type. You have four minutes to discuss. Recorders please write the final idea on the transparency I will give you so we can show all of them on the overhead projector."

Ms. Lewis circulated through the room as the students discussed the idea of a general rule and distributed a strip of transparency (8½ inches wide and about 4 inches high) and a marker pen to each recorder. As she moved from group to group, she basically listened and did not interfere while reminding the recorders to write the result on the transparency.

At the end of four minutes, she called for their attention. She then asked the recorders to bring up their strips and she placed them on the overhead so that each could be seen. "So, here is what you decided as individual groups. Now, take all these ideas and see if you can write a simple way of explaining all of them." Within a few minutes, Melody raised her hand. "Our group said you multiply the number of items by the cost of each item, then do that for the other item and then add those two answers to get a total."

"Great," said Ms. Lewis. "Now, let's look at this idea in measurement." On the overhead project, Ms. Lewis placed a diagram of a rectangle. "Here is a rectangle with sides measuring 7 feet and 3 feet. Let's find the perimeter of this rectangle. To do this, I want someone in the group to look in the back of your notebook to the formula page and make sure your group is using the correct formula. You have two minutes."

After the groups had found the perimeter using the formula $P = 2L + 2W$, Ms. Lewis said, "Now, let's look at Aretha's example from last night's homework and this perimeter example. In your groups one last time, write some ideas about how these two problems are similar."

After about three minutes, Ms. Lewis called on Jocelyn. Jocelyn reported for her group. "They are similar because in each example, you multiply first and then add the answers from the multiplications together."

"Okay," said Ms. Lewis, "Take your notebooks and copy down what Jocelyn said." She had Jocelyn repeat what she had said. "Now, let's be a little more formal."

With this statement, Ms. Lewis put a transparency on the overhead titled: Order of Operations. She said, "From these examples, we see that when we have an addition and a multiplication in the order from these problems, it seems natural from the situation in the problems that we multiply first and then we add. What we have here is the beginning of our study of what is known as the Order of Operations. Right now we have seen what the order is when we have addition and multiplication. Soon, we will look at it for other operations. For tomorrow, your homework will be problems involving purchasing again and some with finding the perimeter of a rectangle. I will pass out the homework. While I do this, get ready to go to Music. Put all your materials in your desk except your math notebook. When you put your homework in your math notebook, put that in your desk also."

## The Mathematics

In many mathematics books, the idea of the order of operations is usually given as a rule with students expected to remember it. I think you can see why students might have trouble with this type of learning. In some textbooks, the order of operations is represented as an agreement among mathematicians. This may not be accurate and certainly does not help the students who again see this as another 'rule' to be remembered.

The order of operations can be seen as the formalized way of looking at what we do in context. Besides the examples in the Activity, we also use the order of operations with place value. For example, if we write 5,736, in a more expanded form we have 5 thousand 7 hundred thirty six.

This can be expanded further to: $5 \times 1000 + 7 \times 100 + 3 \times 10 + 6$ and still further to $5 \times 10^3 + 7 \times 10^2 + 3 \times 10 + 6$. Now, let's look at how we would take the expanded form, $5 \times 10^3 + 7 \times 10^2 + 3 \times 10 + 6$, and evaluate it to produce the standard form. The first operation to be performed is to evaluate the exponents, that is, we change $10^3$ to 1000 and $10^2$ to 100. We cannot do anything to relate the 2nd and 3rd terms ($10^3 + 7$) since they are from different place values. When we evaluate the exponents, we have

$$5 \times 1000 + 7 \times 100 + 3 \times 10 + 6.$$

Then, we perform the three multiplications,

$$5 \times 1000, 7 \times 100 \text{ and } 3 \times 10$$

to get                    $$5000 + 700 + 30 + 6.$$

Then we add to get                    5736.

If we now look at the "order" in which we work, we see that we do the exponents first, then we multiply and then we add. It's the way we work with numbers. So, the order of operation is used in place value and it cannot be an agreement.

Even in simple algebra, when you have $4a^2 + 3a + 7$ and evaluate it for $a = 2$, the first step is to find the value of $a^2$. Sound familiar? Just like the work with base-ten. Work out the evaluation of the algebra if $a = 2$. The answer is at the end of the section.

In fact, there is a geometric idea which can show the natural ideas behind the order of operations. Suppose you have 6 red squares and 7 blue squares. All the red squares have a side of 4 cm and all the blue squares have a side of 2 cm. If you put all the squares together, how many square cm of area do you have?

The first thing to do is to find the area of each square. The area of each red square with the 4 cm side is 16 square cm, that is, $4^2 = 16$. The area of each blue square with a side of 2 cm is 4 square cm.

Next, we now find how many square cm we have for each set of squares.

There are 6 red squares each with an area of 16 sq cm for a total of 96 sq cm ($6 \times 16$).

There are 7 blue squares each with an area of 4 sq. cm for a total of 28 sq cm ($7 \times 4$).

So, the total area is 96 sq cm + 28 sq cm for a sum of 124 sq cm.

Now, let's look at what was done. For each set of squares, we found the area of a single square and then multiplied by the number of squares having that area. For the red squares, this meant $6 \times 4^2$. For the blue squares, this meant $7 \times 2^2$.

The equation for all this is:

$$6 \times 4^2 + 7 \times 2^2 =$$

Evaluating the exponents gives us:   $6 \times 16 + 7 \times 4$

Multiplying gives us           $96 + 28$

And finally adding we get:           $124$

Now, look at what you did first, then second and then third. You evaluated the exponents. Then you multiplied. Then you added. You could not do the problem in any other order. It would not make sense. And the one thing you need to do as a teacher is have the mathematics make sense, even when dealing with the Order of Operations.

(By the way, the answer from the problem above is: If a = 2, then $4a^2 + 3a + 7$ equals 29.)


## The Plan

**Title**: Introduce the order of operations for addition and multiplication.

**Teacher Objective**: To introduce students to the order of operations.

**Objective for Students**: What do you do first?

**NCTM Focal Points 3–5**: Represent, analyze, and generalize a variety of patterns with words and where possible, symbolic rules.

**Materials**: Homework from previous class. "In the newspaper, find items that you wish to buy. Choose two of them and purchase more than one of each. Then find the total cost of your purchase."
Strips of transparency (about 11" long by 4" high)
transparency pens
transparency of a diagram 7" by 3" rectangle

**Homework**: In the newspaper, find items that you wish to buy. Choose two of them and purchase more than one of each. Then find the total cost of your purchase. Find two other sets of items and find the total purchase cost.

Find the perimeter of these rectangles:

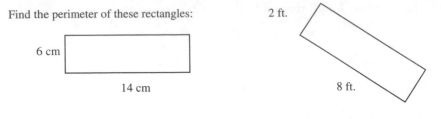

6 cm

14 cm

2 ft.

8 ft.

*Beginning Stage*

1. Review the homework. Have two students read their problems and explain what they did. Have them use the overhead projector.

*Middle Stage*

2. In groups, have students decide on how these types of problems are done.
   a. For this, give each recorder a strip of transparency to have them all fit on overhead at once for analysis.
   b. Have recorders place strips on overhead. Have groups decide how they are similar. Show transparency of rectangle. Ask students to find perimeter. Remind them to check the formula on the formula page in their notebooks.
   c. When students have completed this, have groups compare one of the methods for homework with the method for finding the perimeter.

*Final Stage*

3. Explain that this is called the order of operations.
4. In their notebooks, have them write order of operations and their understanding of what it is.
5. Announce and distribute homework.

**Doing Some Mathematics**

1. Find the total of 3a + 5b where a = 6 and b = 7. What operation did you do first?

2. Mary buys 3 CDs for $8 each and 6 video games for $12 each. Show how you use the order of operations in solving this problem.
3. What number is represented by: $4 \times 10^3 + 8 \times 10^2 + 2 \times 10 + 9$?
4. Use the order of operations to find: $5 \times 3^2 + 6 \times 2^5$.

## Putting It All Together

The order of operations is usually formalized in the upper elementary grades and many times as an arbitrary rule which it is not.

One of the underlying ideas in the lesson here is that in a multiplication, one of the numbers stands for a group of objects or the cost of a single item (quantitative noun) while the other number stands for the number of groups or items (quantitative adjective). So, when there is a choice of multiplication or addition, multiplication is done first. $4 + 5 \times 3$ means 4 is being added to 5 groups of 3. Or, 4 is being added to 15. This in some ways goes back to our discussion of multiplication and its meaning in chapter 4 on skip counting.

This is not a convention as posed in many books. The order of operations is a natural consequence and you as the teacher need to have the students understand this. By their natures, multiplication and addition have the relationship as seem in the Activity. It cannot happen any other way. And why? Because that is the way multiplication is. In doing this, you must keep the actual meaning of multiplication in the forefront of the learning.

## Reflections

*Reflecting on the Activity*

1. How does the approach in this lesson take advantage of mathematics that students know?
2. What do you see as being the most difficult part of the lesson for you?

*Reflecting on the Mathematics*

3. Based on this lesson, what is the order of operations?
4. How would you interpret "2 x 5 + 6 x 3?" How does the meaning of multiplication prevent you from adding the 5 and 6 first?

*Reflecting on the Plan*

5. What do you think yesterday's lesson was about?
6. Why did Ms. Lewis feel comfortable about using examples in which students needed to use the Perimeter formula?

*Your Reflections*

7. Why is it not a good idea to have students rely on "rules" and not understanding in learning mathematics?
8. What types of mathematical ideas were used/reviewed while the students addressed order of operations?
9. Why is it important to integrate topics in mathematics?

# Appendix A

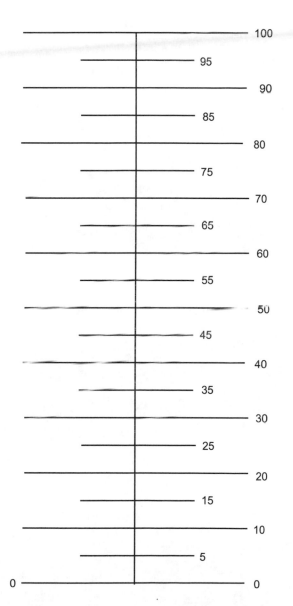

Percent Grid

# Appendix B

Fraction Pieces' Template

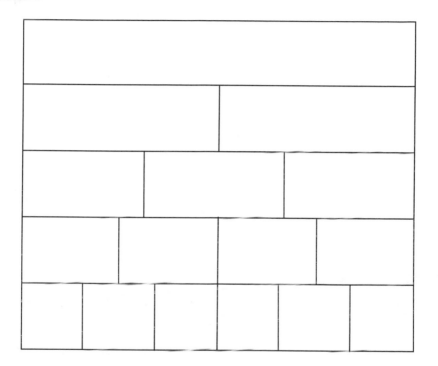

# Bibliography

Adams, D. (1810). *Arithmetic in which the principles operating by numbers are analytically explained and synthetically applied.* Keene, NH: J. & J. W. Prentiss.

Berk, L., & Winsler, A. (1995). *Scaffolding children's learning: Vygotsky and early childhood education.* Washington, D.C.: National Association for the Education of Young Children.

Brown, T. (1997). *Mathematics education and language.* Dordrecht, The Netherlands: Kluwer Academic.

Bruner, J. (1960). *The process of education.* Cambridge, MA: Harvard University Press.

Cocking, R., & Mestre, J. (Eds.). (1998). *Linguistic and cultural influences on learning mathematics.* Hillsdale, NJ: Erlbaum.

Dienes, Z. (1963). *An experimental study of mathematics-learning.* London: Hutchinson.

French, J. (1869). *Common school arithmetic.* New York: Harper Brothers.

Gardella, F., & Tong, V. (2002, August). Linguistic considerations in the acquisition and teaching of mathematics. *WORD, Journal of the International Linguistics Association, 53*(2).

Groesbeck, J. (1885). *Crittenden commercial arithmetic and business manual.* Philadelphia: Eldredge & Brother.

Howson, A. G. (1983). Language and the teaching of mathematics. In M. Zweng et al. (Eds.), *Proceedings of the fourth international congress on mathematical education* (pp. 568–573). Boston: Birkhauser.

Lederer, R. (1991). *The miracle of language.* New York: Pocket Books.

National Council of Teachers of Mathematics. (1980). *Agenda for action.* Reston, VA: Author.

National Council of Teachers of Mathematics. (2000). *Principles and standards for school mathematics.* Reston, VA: Author.

National Council of Teachers of Mathematics. (1989). *Standards for curriculum and evaluation in school mathematics.* Reston, VA: Author.

Owens, R. E., Jr. (1984). *Language development: An introduction* (2nd ed.). Princeton, NC: Merrill.

Pinker, S. (1994). *The language instinct: How the mind creates language.* New York: William Morrow.

Pulaski, M. A. S. (1971). *Understanding Piaget: An introduction to children's cognitive development.* New York: Harper & Row.

Sousa, D. (2006). *How the brain learns* (3rd ed.). Thousand Oaks, CA: Corwin Press.

Sousa, D. (2008). *How the brain learns mathematics.* Thousand Oaks, CA: Corwin Press.

# Index